FEDERAL INCOME TAXATION OF BUSINESS ORGANIZATIONS

FIFTH EDITION

STUDY PROBLEMS

by

MARTIN J. MCMAHON, JR.
Professor of Law and
James J. Freeland Eminent Scholar in Taxation
University of Florida

DANIEL L. SIMMONS
Professor of Law Emeritus
University of California at Davis

444 Cedar Street, Suite 700
St. Paul, MN 55101
1-877-888-1330

Printed in the United States of America

ISBN: 978-1-60930-196-5

Mat #41312944

PREFACE

This problem set is designed to accompany our casebook, *Federal Income Taxation of Business Organizations*, Fifth Edition, although the problems can be used with any other text. The problems are organized to correspond with the Chapter and section headings of our casebook. Each problem may be answered by reference to the Internal Revenue Code, the applicable Treasury regulations, and the material in the corresponding section of the casebook. In general, the solution to each problem can be found within the material presented in the corresponding section of the casebook.

At various times, one or the other of us has used the relevant portions of these problems in two and three semester hour classes on the taxation of partnerships, and sometimes Subchapter S corporations, four semester hour courses on taxation of Corporations, a three hour course on taxation of acquisitions and reorganizations, and a four hour combined course on the taxation of partnerships and corporations that incorporates the material in Chapters 1 through 17 of the casebook. Both the casebook and this problem set are structured so that an instructor may organize a course consisting of various Chapters and sections in any order that the instructor may choose.

This problem set also can be correlated with the Chapters and section organization of our companion books, *Federal Income Taxation of Partnerships and S Corporations*, and *Federal Income Taxation of Corporations*. The chapter numbers of the partnership book are the same as the numbering of Chapters 1 through 9 of this problem set. The Chapter 1 of *Taxation of Corporations* corresponds to Chapter 10 of this problem set. Foundation Press also publishes separate editions of these problems that correspond to *Federal Income Taxation of Partnerships and S Corporations*, and *Federal Income Taxation of Corporations*.

MARTIN J. MCMAHON, JR.
DANIEL L. SIMMONS

June 2014

TABLE OF CONTENTS

PART I

Taxation of Partners and Partnerships

CHAPTER 1

INTRODUCTION TO PARTNERSHIP TAXATION

SECTION 2. DEFINITION OF A PARTNERSHIP

A. PARTNERSHIP VERSUS CORPORATION

1. Anne and Bill plan to form a limited liability company to engage in the business of developing and marketing computer software. They have identified between 35 and 50 potential investors who will contribute varying amounts of cash for membership interests totaling approximately 75% - 85% of profits and losses (after Anne and Bill receive handsome salaries). Under the governing state law, the LLC may be member-managed or manager-managed, membership interests may be freely transferable or nontransferable, and the LLC may or may

not be dissolved by the death, bankruptcy, retirement, or expulsion of a member, all as provided in the LLC agreement. Anne and Bill want the LLC to be managed by themselves, with the investors having only the minimal rights of members required by state law. Only Anne and Bill will have authority to act on behalf of the LLC. Because of the limited powers that the investor-members will be granted, Anne and Bill think it best that the investors be permitted to sell or assign their membership interests if they so desire, although Anne and Bill think that the actual opportunities for resale will be limited by market forces. Of course, Anne and Bill want the business of the LLC to be uninterrupted by the death, bankruptcy, etc. of an investor-member. Will the LLC be taxed as a partnership or as a corporation if organized in the manner contemplated by Anne and Bill?

2. X Corporation operates a children's toy business and manufactures automatic weapons. In order to separate potential liabilities, X Corporation forms a limited liability company, Guns-Я-Us LLC, to which it transfers the weapons manufacturing operation. What is the tax status of the Gus-Я-Us LLC?

B. PARTNERSHIP VERSUS OTHER BUSINESS ARRANGEMENT

1. Suphuric Electric Power Co. and the Metropolis Municipal Electric Co. own a coal mine in Kentucky as tenants in common. Each of them pays one-half of the costs of operating the mine and is entitled to take one-half of the output for use in their respective electric generating businesses, which are otherwise unrelated. Are Suphuric Electric Power Co. and the Metropolis Municipal Electric Co. partners with respect to the coal mine operation?

2. Glenn and Helen are lawyers who share a single office suite and secretary. Glenn is a real estate lawyer and Helen is a plaintiff's trial lawyer. They share general overhead office expenses (e.g., office rent and utilities, computer and photocopier lease, etc.) but each pays his or her own share of variable expenses, (e.g., long distance telephone calls, travel, etc.) and they service and bill their own clients. They do, however, refer clients to each other from time to time for work within the other's area of expertise. Are they partners for tax purposes?

3. Al, Betty, Carl and Donna purchased Blackacre, which is 500 acres of undeveloped land on the outskirts of Gotham City, as tenants in common. Each contributed $100,000 toward the purchase price.

(a) They plan to hold Blackacre as a speculative investment for several years, until Gotham City expands and Blackacre appreciates, and hope then to sell it to an as of now undetermined real estate developer. Have Al, Betty, Carl and Donna formed a partnership? Would it make any difference if they agreed that none of them would have a right to sell his or her undivided interest in Blackacre independently of the others?

(b) Al, Betty, Carl and Donna hire a surveyor to prepare a subdivision plat for Blackacre, which they plan to divide into 200 house lots. Al Betty, Carl, and Donna sell the lots in differing numbers to 20 different builders and split the profits equally. Have Al, Betty, Carl and Donna formed a partnership? Would it make any difference if they planned to sell all of the subdivision lots to one builder, but obtained the subdivision approval first in order to increase the value of the entire tract?

4. (a) Ed and Fay each contributed $500,000 to the purchase price of a 30 unit apartment building. Is there any way that Ed and Fay can avoid being classified as a partnership if they operate the apartment building?

   (b) What if the property Ed and Fay bought was a warehouse with a single tenant under a 20 year lease?

   (c) What if Ed and Fay are husband and wife who reside in California, a community property state?

5. Ilene purchased a vacant apartment building and agreed with Jake, who is an architect-contractor, that if Jake would supervise the renovation of the apartment building for sale as condominium units, Jake would be entitled to 30 percent of the profits from the resale. Are Ilene and Jake partners for federal income tax purposes? Is whether Jake shares losses relevant? Is whether Jake has a voice in determining the nature of the renovation, the costs to be incurred, and the sales price asked for the condominium units relevant?

6. Kyle graduated from M.I.T. and started an unincorporated computer software development business. To finance development of a new software program, Kyle borrowed $1,000,000 from the Pari-Mutual Venture Capital Fund. The loan is evidenced by a nonrecourse promissory note due in 10 years. Interest is set at the prime rate plus 10% per year, plus 30% of Kyle's net profits from the exploitation of the software. Are Kyle and Pari-Mutual Venture Capital Fund partners?

7. A owns the X LLC; A and X LLC formed the AX LLC. Is the AX LLC a partnership for federal income tax purposes?

CHAPTER 2

FORMATION OF THE PARTNERSHIP

SECTION 1. CONTRIBUTIONS OF MONEY OR PROPERTY

1. Amy, Bill, and Casey are forming a limited liability company (that will be taxed as a partnership) to conduct a bait and tackle shop, fishing guide, and marina business on the Intracoastal Waterway. Each of them will have an equal interest in capital and profits. Each partner will transfer the following assets:

Partner	Asset	Adjusted Basis	FMV
Amy:	Marina:		
	Land	$10,000	$40,000
	Buildings	$30,000	$60,000
	Tradename "Shark Bait"	$ 1,000	$10,000
Bill:	Store Fixtures (§ 1245 recomputed basis = $50,000)	$25,000	$45,000
	Inventory	$34,000	$65,000
Casey:	Fishing Boat	$30,000	$20,000
	Accounts Receivable	$ 0	$ 5,000
	Cash	$85,000	$85,000

Amy and Casey previously conducted their respective sole proprietorships using the cash method of accounting; Bill used the accrual method.

(a) At what values should the contributed property be carried on the partnership's books and what is the amount of each partner's capital account?

(b) What are the tax consequences of the formation of the partnership? What is each partner's basis for his or her partnership interest? What is the partnership's basis in each asset?

(c) If the partnership sells the inventory contributed by Bill for $65,000 and collects $5,000 on the accounts receivable contributed by Casey, how will the partners be taxed?

(d) If the partnership sells the inventory contributed by Bill for $80,000, how will the partners be taxed?

(e) If the partnership sells the fishing boat for $20,000, how will the partners be taxed?

(f) If the partnership sells the fishing boat for $17,000, how will the partners be taxed?

2. Dana and Ed are forming a limited partnership to engage in the real estate development business. Dana, a real estate agent, will be the general partner; Ed, a dentist, will be the limited partner. Dana will contribute an installment promissory note, with a basis of $50,000 and a face amount of $100,000, which was received on the sale of land held for speculative investment, in exchange for a one quarter interest in partnership profits and capital. Ed will contribute Blackacre, which has a basis of $50,000 and a fair market value of $125,000, and Whiteacre, which has a basis of $200,000 and a fair market value of $175,000, in exchange for a three-quarters interest in profits and capital. Dana, Ed, and the partnership are cash method taxpayers.

(a) At what values should the contributed property be carried on the partnership's books and what will be the amount of each partner's capital account?

(b) What are the tax consequences of the formation of the partnership? What is each partner's basis for his or her partnership interest? What is the partnership's basis in Blackacre and Whiteacre?

(c)(1) How are the partners taxed when the partnership collects the installment note?

(2) What is the character of the gain when the partnership sells Blackacre and Whiteacre? Does it matter how long Ed held the contributed property?

(3) What would be the amount of loss recognized if Whiteacre had been Ed's residential farm property prior to its contribution to the partnership and the partnership sold it for $165,000?

SECTION 2. CONTRIBUTIONS OF ENCUMBERED PROPERTY

1. Fran, George, and Helen formed the FGH General Partnership. Each of them has a one-third interest in partnership capital, profits, and losses. Fran and George each contributed $20,000 cash to the FGH Partnership and Helen contributed Greenacre, which is worth $50,000 and subject to a mortgage of $30,000, which was assumed by the partnership.

   (a) Assume that each partner would be responsible for one-third of the debt if the partnership's assets were worthless.

   (1) Ignoring the tax consequences, if the value of Greenacre is unchanged, what happens to the partners if Greenacre is sold, the debt is paid, and all partnership proceeds are distributed to the partners?

   (2) What are the tax consequences if Helen's basis in Greenacre was $35,000?

   (3) What are the tax consequences if Helen's basis in Greenacre was $15,000?

   (b) Assume that the mortgage debt is nonrecourse as to both Helen and the FGH Partnership.

   (1) Ignoring tax consequences, if the value of Greenacre is unchanged, what happens to the partners if Greenacre is sold, the debt is paid, and all partnership proceeds are distributed to the partners?

   (2) What are the tax consequences if Helen's basis in Greenacre was $40,000?

   (3) What are the tax consequences if Helen's basis in Greenacre was $15,000?

2. Lisa, who previously has conducted a solo medical practice, joined a partnership with two other physicians. Each partner has a one-third interest. Lisa transferred $18,000 of accounts receivable from her solo practice to the partnership, which assumed $12,000 of Lisa's accounts payable.

   (a) What are the tax consequences of the transaction if Lisa and the partnership use the cash method of accounting?

(b) What are the tax consequences of the transaction if Lisa and the partnership use the accrual method of accounting?

SECTION 3. CONTRIBUTION OF PROPERTY VERSUS CONTRIBUTION OF SERVICES

A. TREATMENT OF THE PARTNER RECEIVING A PARTNERSHIP INTEREST IN EXCHANGE FOR SERVICES

1. Avery and Blair each hold a fifty percent interest in the AB LLC, a limited liability company taxed as a partnership. The sole asset of the AB LLC is Blackacre, a 1,000 acre farm worth $1,200,000. AB LLC purchased Blackacre several years ago for $900,000, and that amount is its current adjusted basis. Avery and Blair each have a basis in their interests in the LLC (from cash contributions) of $450,000. Avery and Blair have offered Charlie a one-third interest in the LLC capital and profits (which would reduce Avery's and Blair's interests from one-half each to one-third each).

   Determine the tax consequences to Charlie under each of the following situations:

   (a) Charlie is a lawyer and receives the one-third interest valued at $400,000 in consideration of legal services previously rendered to the LLC in defending it against an "attractive nuisance" suit by a trespasser injured on the Blackacre premises.

   (b) Charlie is an architect who owns plans for an apartment building drawn for a project that never was undertaken. Charlie will supervise construction of an apartment building on the land using the plans. Avery, Blair, and Charlie value Charlie's contribution at $600,000 and provide him with a capital account in that amount.

   (c) Charlie receives the interest in exchange for agreeing to act for four years as the manager of an apartment complex that will be built on the land. (Assume that Avery and Blair each will contribute one-half of the cash necessary to build the apartment complex.) If, however, Charlie quits working for the LLC during the four-year period, the interest will be forfeited. Are the value and basis of Blackacre (or any of the LLC assets) at the end of year four relevant to your answer?

2. Block & Eggers, C.P.A. is a certified public accounting firm with 50 general partners. Dana, who has been an employee of the firm for 10 years, finally has been admitted to the partnership this year. Dana's opening capital account is fixed at zero, but Dana will share in all profits and losses following admission to the partnership. Is Dana's

admission to the partnership a taxable event? What if the partnership is on the cash method of accounting and Dana is entitled to a share of any accounts receivable outstanding on the day of admission to the partnership?

3. Elliot is the investment manager for Pari-Mutual Capital Associates, a limited partnership, which has nearly one hundred partners (but which is not publicly traded). Elliot received a nonforfeitable, one percent, profits-only limited partnership interest in the partnership, whose assets consist of a portfolio of New York Stock Exchange traded securities with a value of $100,000,000, as a bonus for his many years of faithful service to the partnership in managing its portfolio of investments. Income from the portfolio has been averaging $5,000,000 per year for the last five years. What are the tax consequences to Elliot upon receipt of the profits interest? Should *Diamond* apply? Should § 83 apply?

B. TREATMENT OF THE PARTNERSHIP ISSUING A PARTNERSHIP INTEREST FOR SERVICES

1. (a) In problem 1(a) of Part A, what is the tax consequence to the AB LLC on the receipt of Charlie's legal services in exchange for admitting Charlie to the partnership as a one-third partner with a $400,000 capital account?

   (b) Does your answer change if Avery and Blair hold Blackacre as joint tenants in an arrangement that is not treated as a partnership, then create an LLC with Charlie? Avery and Blair contribute their joint tenancy interest in Blackacre for a one-third interest each. Charlie receives a one-third interest in the LLC in exchange for his legal services.

2. In problem 1(b) of Part A, what is the tax consequence to the AB LLC on the receipt of Charlie's services in exchange for admitting Charlie to the partnership as a one-third partner with a $600,000 capital account?

CHAPTER 3

Taxation of Partnership Taxable Income to the Partners

Section 1. Pass-Thru of Partnership Income and Loss

1. Sean and Terry are partners in an investment partnership. Sean's share of partnership profits and losses is two-thirds and Terry's share is one-third. Sean, Terry, and the partnership are all cash method calendar year taxpayers. For the current year the partnership received or incurred the following items.

Receipts and Gains:	
Rents	$300,000
Gain from the sale of used computer (§ 1245 gain)	$ 3,000
Gain from sale of apartment building (§ 1231 gain)	$150,000
Short Term Capital Gain on NYSE traded securities	$ 12,000
Long Term Capital Gain on sale of land held for speculative investment	$ 90,000
Interest on City of New York bonds	$ 3,000

Outlays and Losses:	
Employee salaries	$ 30,000
Rent	$ 24,000
Depreciation (ACRS)	$ 15,000
Stock broker's fees	$ 3,000
Charitable contributions	$ 9,000
Legal fees incurred to lobby Congress to reduce the tax rate on capital gains	$ 4,500
Long Term Capital Loss on sale of land held for speculative investment	$ 60,000
Short Term Capital Loss on NYSE traded securities	$ 9,000

(a)(1) How should the partnership, Sean, and Terry report these items? Does it matter whether the partnership makes any distributions?

(2) Would your answer change if Terry's primary occupation was as a dealer in real estate and most sales of land owned by him individually resulted in ordinary income characterization?

(b) Assume that the basis of Sean's partnership interest at the beginning of the year was $200,000 and the basis of Terry's partnership interest at the beginning of the year was $100,000. What are their bases in their respective partnership interests at the end of the year?

(c) What would be the tax consequences if the partnership distributed $20,000 to Sean and $10,000 to Terry on the last day of every month during the taxable year?

2. This year the Merrill, Barney & Dean partnership sold a parcel of investment real estate with a basis of $100,000 for $700,000. The partnership received a $150,000 down payment and the purchaser's 10-year promissory note (with interest, compounded semi-annually, at the mid-term federal rate) for $550,000. On the partnership's return, the sale was properly treated as an installment sale under § 453. As a result of transactions unrelated to the partnership, Dean had a significant capital loss carryover to this year and prefers to elect-out of § 453 installment sale treatment under § 453(c). May Dean separately elect out of § 453?

3. Several years ago, Mike and Nora formed a general partnership to purchase, rehabilitate, and rent multifamily residences. Mike contributed $200,000 in cash and Nora contributed $100,000 in cash. Mike is a two-thirds partner and Nora is a one-third partner. The partnership has made no distributions. At end of the year, the partnership held the following assets, at fair market value, book value, and basis:

Asset	F.M.V.	Book Value	Basis
Cash	$120,000	$120,000	$120,000
Blackacre	$150,000	$ 90,000	$ 90,000
Whiteacre	$240,000	$180,000	$180,000
Greenacre	$ 60,000	$ 75,000	$ 75,000

The partnership has no debts. Can you ascertain each of Mike's and Nora's respective bases in their partnership interests?

4. What taxable year may the partnership adopt in each of the following situations?

(a) The partnership is a real estate rental business conducted by 10 individuals, all of whom report on the calendar-year.

(b) The partnership runs a ski resort in Colorado, which is open from November through April, with most of its business in January and February, and consists of three calendar-year individuals.

(c) The partnership operates a coal mine. Two of its partners are electric power utility companies, Carbonic Power Co. and Sulphuric Electric Power Co. What is the taxable year of the partnership if:

(1) Both power companies are 30 percent partners and report on an April 30th fiscal year. All of the remaining partners are individuals.

(2) Both power companies are 25 percent partners and report on an April 30 fiscal year. All of the remaining partners are individuals.

(3) Both power companies are 25 percent partners. Carbonic Power Company reports on an April 30th fiscal year and Sulphuric Electric Power reports on a September 30th fiscal year. All of the remaining partners are individuals.

(d)(1) The partnership operates a coal mine. It has three equal corporate general partners. Two partners report on a May 31st fiscal year and one partner reports on a November 30th fiscal year.

(2) What taxable year would be required if the partner on a November 30th fiscal year purchased the entire interest of one of the other two partners?

SECTION 2. LIMITATION ON PARTNERS' DEDUCTIONS OF PARTNERSHIP LOSSES

1. Gill and Harriet are general partners who share income and losses equally. Gill's basis in his partnership interest is $7,000 and Harriet's basis in her partnership interest is $12,000.

   (a) During the current year the partnership incurs an operating loss of $20,000. How much loss can each of Gill and Harriet claim on their individual returns? What are their respective bases in their partnership interests after taking into account their shares of partnership losses?

   (b) In the following year the partnership realized no operating income, but did recognize a $5,000 long-term capital gain. What are the consequences to the partners in that year?

(c) What are the results if in the current year, in which the partnership incurred a $20,000 loss, between January 1st and December 30th the partnership distributed $4,000 in cash to each of Gill and Harriet?

(d) Gill died on January 1st of the year following the year in which the loss was incurred, and his wife, Irene, inherited his partnership interest. What would be the tax consequences to Irene if the partnership recognized a $5,000 long-term capital gain in that year?

CHAPTER 4

DETERMINING PARTNERS' DISTRIBUTIVE SHARES

SECTION 2. THE 704(b) REGULATIONS

A. ALLOCATIONS OF ITEMS UNRELATED TO NONRECOURSE DEBT

(1) ECONOMIC EFFECT

1. Al and Brett each contributed $320,000 to form a general partnership, which purchased a parcel of land for $40,000 and constructed an office building for $600,000. Assume that the property has a 30 year cost recovery period under § 168 and the depreciation method is straight-line. Thus, the annual depreciation deduction is $20,000. The partnership's annual rental income exactly equals its deductible cash flow operating expenses, with the result that net partnership taxable income for each year is a loss of $20,000. The partnership agreement allocates all items of income and loss equally, except the depreciation deductions, which are allocated entirely to Brett. Both partners are unconditionally obligated to restore any deficit to their capital accounts upon a liquidation of the partnership.

   (a) What additional provisions must be included in the partnership agreement for the allocation of depreciation to be respected?

   (b) (1) What should be the amount in each partner's capital account at the end of the third year of partnership operations?

   (2) At the end of 17 years of operations?

   (c)(1) If the partnership sold the land and building for $660,000 on the first day of the fourth year and then liquidated, how must the proceeds be distributed?

   (2) What if the sales price was $540,000?

   (d) Will the allocations qualify if the partnership agreement contains a "gain chargeback," which allocates first to Brett the portion of any gain on a sale that equals the depreciation deductions specially allocated to her? Assume that the partnership sells the building on January 1 of year four for $660,000, and, alternatively, for $540,000.

(e) Will the allocations qualify if the partnership agreement provides that all nonliquidating distributions are to be made 60 percent to Al and 40 percent to Brett?

(f) Assume that the partnership is a limited partnership, with Al as the general partner and Brett as the limited partner. As a limited partner, Brett is not required to restore a deficit in her capital account, but as the general partner Al is required to restore a deficit capital account.

(1) May depreciation deductions be specially allocated to Brett? If so, for how many years? How must the depreciation deductions be allocated in the 17th year of partnership operations?

(2) How would your answer change if at the end of the sixteenth year Brett contributed her promissory note for $160,000 to the partnership?

2. What would be the result in each of problems 1.(a) - (d) if Al and Brett each contributed $30,000 to form the general partnership and the partnership borrowed $580,000 to purchase the land and construct the building?

3. What would be the result in problem 1.(f) if Al and Brett each contributed $30,000 to form the limited partnership and the partnership borrowed $580,000 to purchase the land and construct the building?

4. Luke, Mona, and Nikita will form the LMN LLC. Luke will contribute $30,000,000 in cash. Mona will contribute $10,000,000 in cash. Nikita will contribute intellectual property with a basis of zero and speculative, if any, market value, but Nikita will agree to work full time running the business of the LMN LLC. Luke and Mona are simply investors. Nikita will be the managing member; Luke and Mona will be non-managing members. Luke will receive one Class A LLC unit, one Class B LLC unit, and one Class C LLC unit. Mona will receive one Class B LLC unit and one Class C LLC unit. Nikita will receive one Class C LLC unit. The Class A LLC unit (Luke) will be entitled to the first $20,000,000 upon liquidation of the LMN LLC. Upon liquidation of the LLC, after satisfaction of the $30,000,000 liquidation preference of the Class A LLC unit, the Class B LLC units (Luke and Mona) will share equally the next $20,000,000, with the amount due to each unit to be reduced proportionately if the LMN LLC's assets are insufficient to distribute $10,000,000 with respect to each unit. The Class A LLC unit will be entitled to the first $1,500,000

of annual partnership profits (5%). The two Class B LLC units will share equally the next $1,200,000 of annual partnership profits (6%) after the $1,500,000 allocated to the Class A unit. To the extent the Class A and Class B units' shares of annual income have not been distributed prior to liquidation, after the $20,000,000 attributable to the contributions for Class B units have been satisfied, first, the preferential liquidation distribution due to the Class A unit will be increased by the undistributed amount of profits allocated to it, and, second, the preferential liquidation distribution due to the Class B units will be increased by the undistributed amount of profits allocated to then. After satisfaction of the preferential annual allocations to the Class A and Class B units, the three Class C units share the LMN LLC's residual profits and losses equally. Losses will be allocated first against income allocated to the Class C units, then against income allocated to the Class B units, and then against income allocated to the Class A units. Losses in excess of cumulative profits are allocated first to the Class B units to the extent of the liquidation preference of the Class B units ($20,000,000, then against the liquidation preference of the Class A units. No member of the LLC will be required to make any contribution to the LMN LLC beyond the initial contribution. Do the Code and regulations allow a partnership agreement to be written so as to achieve these goals and have the allocations of profits and losses be respected in whole or in part?

(2) SUBSTANTIALITY

1. Carlos and Diana formed a general partnership to invest in a small commercial office building. Each contributed $100,000 to the partnership which also borrowed $800,000 from the First State Bank to acquire a building for $1,000,000. Unfortunately Carlos and Diana purchased their building at the height of the real estate boom. One year after the investment the value of the building declined to $600,000 and the rental income was insufficient to meet payments on the loan. In addition, Carlos, but not Diana, was insolvent. First State Bank agreed to reduce the loan principal to $600,000. Diana contributed $5,000 to the EF partnership to pay the costs of the loan adjustment. Because of Diana's capital contribution, the EF partnership revalued its capital accounts to fair market value pursuant to Treas. Reg. § 1.704-1(b)(2)(iv)(f). Carlos and Diana also amended their partnership agreement to allocate the $5,000 expenditure to Diana, allocate the revaluation loss $300,000 to Carlos and $100,000 to Diana, and to allocate discharge of indebtedness income to Carlos. The partnership agreement provides for properly maintained capital accounts and for liquidation distributions to be made in accord with the capital accounts. There is no provision for a deficit make-up. Do these allocations have substantial economic effect?

2. (a) Eddie and Fran formed a general partnership to operate an adventure vacation tour company, offering hunting, fishing, and whitewater rafting in the Canadian and U.S. Rocky Mountains. Eddie is a Canadian resident; Fran is a U.S. resident. The partnership agreement provides that the partners' capital accounts will be maintained as required by the § 704(b) regulations, liquidating distributions will be made in accordance with the partners' capital account balances, and any partner must restore a negative capital account upon liquidation. The partnership agreement provides that Eddie will be allocated 80 percent and Fran 20 percent of the income or loss from Canadian trips, and Fran will be allocated 80 percent and Eddie 20 percent of the income or loss from U.S. trips. The amount of income or loss from each source cannot be predicted with any reasonable certainty. Do these allocations have substantial economic effect?

   (b) Assume the same facts as in (a) except that the partnership agreement provides that all income or loss will be shared equally, but that Eddie will be allocated all income or loss derived from Canadian operations as a part of his equal share of partnership income or loss, up to the amount of that share. As a result of this allocation, the total tax liability of Eddie and Fran for each year to which these allocations relate will be reduced. Do these allocations have substantial economic effect?

3. Gail and Haley formed a partnership to develop and market computer software. Gail contributed $10,000 in cash and Haley contributed $200,000. The partnership agreement provides that all § 174 deductions for research and experimental expenditures are to be allocated to Haley. In addition, Haley will be allocated 90 percent, and Gail 10 percent, of all partnership income or loss, excluding research and experimental expenditures, until Haley has received aggregate allocations of income equal to the sum of such research and experimental expenditures and his share of such taxable loss. Thereafter, Gail and Haley will share all taxable income and loss equally. Operating cash flow will be distributed equally between Gail and Haley. The partnership agreement also provides that Gail's and Haley's capital accounts will be determined and maintained in accordance with the § 704(b) regulations, liquidating distributions will be made in accordance with the partners' capital account balances, and that upon liquidation partners must restore deficit capital account balances. Do these allocations have substantial economic effect?

B. ALLOCATIONS ATTRIBUTABLE TO NONRECOURSE DEBT

1. Charlie is the general partner and Denise and Ella are the limited partners of the CDE limited partnership. Charlie contributed $10,000

and Denise and Ella each contributed $45,000 in cash. The initial contribution was used to purchase a parcel of land for $100,000. The partnership then borrowed $1,200,000 from an unrelated commercial lender on a nonrecourse basis to construct an office building to be held for rental. The loan requires only interest payments for 10 years, at the end of which time the full principal balance is due. The partnership agreement allocates all income, gain, loss, and deductions 10 percent to Charlie and 45 percent to each of Denise and Ella until the partnership cumulatively has recognized items of income and gain that equal its recognized items of deduction and loss. Thereafter, all partnership items will be allocated 20 percent to Charlie and 40 percent to each of Denise and Ella. The partnership agreement requires that capital accounts be properly maintained and that the partnership will be liquidated according to capital account balances. Only Charlie, the general partner, is required to restore a capital account deficit, but the partnership agreement contains a "qualified income offset" and a "minimum gain chargeback" provision. Rental income from the property equals deductible cash flow operating expenses. Assume that the property has a 30 year cost recovery period. Thus, annual taxable income is a net operating loss of $40,000.

(a) What is the significance of the "qualified income offset" and "minimum gain chargeback" provisions?

(b) How will the partnership's depreciation deductions be allocated among the partners for each of the first four years of the partnership?

(c) How would the partnership's depreciation deductions be allocated among the partners for each of the first four years of the partnership if the partnership agreement provided that Charlie would be allocated 2 percent and Denise and Ella each would be allocated 49 percent of the partnership's depreciation deductions, but all other items would be allocated as in the basic facts?

2. Amy, Bill, and Casey are forming a limited liability company (that will be taxed as a partnership) to conduct a restaurant business in a leased building. Each of them will contribute $100,000 in cash to purchase furniture and equipment and to provide start-up working capital. Each of them will have an equal interest in the capital and profits of the LLC. Is it important that the LLC agreement comply with the alternative test for substantial economic effect provided in Treas. Reg. § 1.704-1(b)(2)(i)(d)?

SECTION 3. ALLOCATIONS WITH RESPECT TO CONTRIBUTED PROPERTY

1. Sean and Pat formed a general partnership to which Sean contributed $50,000 of cash and Pat contributed depreciable property with a fair market value of $50,000 and a basis of $30,000. The property had a ten-year cost recovery period, of which 5 years were remaining on the contribution date; it is being depreciated under the straight-line method. The partnership agreement provides that Sean and Pat will share profits and losses equally. Each year the partnership recognized $12,000 of gross income and no deductions other than the depreciation deductions on the contributed property.

   (a) How much depreciation will be allocated to Sean and Pat respectively for book and tax purposes?

   (b)(1) If the property contributed by Pat is sold for $30,000 after it has been held by the partnership for two years, how will the partnership allocate the gain for book and tax purposes?

   (2) If the property contributed by Pat is sold for $60,000 after it has been held by the partnership for two years, how will the partnership allocate the gain for book and tax purposes?

   (3) If the property contributed by Pat is sold for $15,000 after it has been held by the partnership for five years and is fully depreciated, how will the partnership allocate the gain for book and tax purposes?

2. The basic facts of Problem 1. apply, but assume that Pat's basis for the depreciable property was only $20,000.

   (a) How much depreciation will be allocated to Sean and Pat respectively for book and tax purposes if the partnership applies the "traditional method" with the ceiling rule?

   (b) How will the partnership allocate depreciation and partnership gross income, for both book and tax purposes, if the partnership elects to use "curative allocations?"

   (c) How will the partnership allocate depreciation and partnership gross income, for both book and tax purposes, if the partnership elects to use "remedial allocations?"

3. Todd and Ursula are partners in the TU Partnership which owns Greenacre, a farm that is leased to tenant farmers. The fair market value of Greenacre is $1,200,000, its basis and book value to the

partnership is $600,000. Todd and Ursula each have a $300,000 basis in their partnership interests. Veronica joins the partnership by contributing Whiteacre which has a fair market value of $600,000. Veronica's basis in Whiteacre is $700,000. Todd, Ursula, and Veronica will share all profits and losses one-third each. On Veronica's admission to the partnership the partnership will revalue its assets to fair market value. What are the tax consequences to the partnership and the partners from the sale of Whiteacre in each of the following circumstances?

(a) One year after Veronica joins the partnership the TUV partnership sells Whiteacre for $540,000.

(b) One year after Veronica joins the partnership, the TUV partnership sells Greenacre for $1,200,000 and distributes $600,000 cash to Veronica who leaves the partnership. The $600,000 of partnership tax gain on the sale of Greenacre is properly allocated $300,000 each to Todd and Ursula. Veronica recognizes a $100,000 loss on her liquidation distribution. In the next taxable year the partnership sells Whiteacre for $540,000.

4 Kim and Lesley each contributed $150,000 to form a limited liability company that is taxed as a partnership. They shared profits and losses equally. Using the initial contribution, the K&L LLC purchased an apartment building and began to renovate it for sale as condominiums. When Kim and Lesley were unable to finish the project, Marion was admitted as a new member of the LLC in consideration of a $250,000 cash contribution to fund completion of the project. At the time Marion was admitted to membership in the LLC, the fair market value of the building project, which was the LLC's sole asset, was $500,000.

(a) What would be the result if the capital account and allocation provisions of the LLC agreement were not amended to reflect Marion's admission as a member?

(b) How should the capital account and allocation provisions of the LLC agreement be amended to reflect Marion's admission as a member? Assume that after completion of the project using Marion's contribution, all of the condominium units were sold in the same year for an aggregate price of $1,200,000, resulting in a taxable profit of $650,000.

SECTION 5. ALLOCATIONS WHERE INTERESTS VARY DURING THE YEAR

1. Prior to October 1st, Nora and Oliver were equal partners in a general partnership. As of October 1st, Pat made a capital contribution to the partnership and the partnership agreement was amended to make Nora, Oliver, and Pat equal partners. During the year the partnership recognized $180,000 of net income from business operations. Net operating income of $90,000 was realized in January through September, and net operating income of $90,000 was realized in October through December. In addition, in November, the partnership sold an item of § 1231 property and recognized a $60,000 loss. The partnership uses the accrual method and is on the calendar year.

   (a) How much income and loss must each partner include under the closing of the books method?

   (b) How much income and loss must each partner include under the proration method?

   (c) When is it likely that the partners will decide whether to elect to use the proration method?

2. Ursula and Vanessa were equal partners in a partnership that used the cash method of accounting and calendar year. Last year the partnership reported no taxable income or loss; however, it incurred a $90,000 expense item that was not paid, but would have been deductible if it had been paid. On June 1st of this year William made a capital contribution to become a one-third partner. This year the partnership earned net taxable income of $36,000, at the rate of $3,000 per month, and in August it paid the $90,000 expense item.

   (a) What is each partner's distributive share of income or loss for this year using the closing of the books method?

   (b) What is each partner's distributive share of income or loss for this year using the proration method?

CHAPTER 5

ALLOCATION OF PARTNERSHIP LIABILITIES

SECTION 1. ALLOCATION OF RECOURSE LIABILITES

1. Sean and Pat formed a general partnership. Sean contributed $50,000 split profits and losses equally. The partnership borrowed $100,000 from Cottage Savings Bank on a recourse basis. What is the basis of each of Sean and Pat in their partnership interests?

2. David and Ruth formed a general partnership to which they each contributed $50,000 in cash. They agreed to split profits equally, but losses were to be allocated 60 percent to David and 40 percent to Ruth. The partnership borrowed $100,000 from Hillsboro National Bank on a recourse basis. What is the basis of each of David and Ruth in their partnership interests?

3. Juan, Kimberly, and Maurice form a partnership to invest in commercial real estate. Kimberly and Maurice each contribute $50,000 in cash to the partnership. Juan forms a Limited Liability Company, in which he is the sole member. The LLC's assets are limited to $90,000 of cash. The Juan LLC contributes $50,000 of cash to the JKM partnership. The partnership borrows $1,000,000 with full recourse to the partnership and purchases an office building for $1,150,000. The partners share all partnership items equally, one-third each. The partnership agreement provides for properly maintained capital accounts, liquidation in accord with capital accounts, and that each partner is responsible for repayment of the partner's capital account deficit, if any. What is each partner's basis in the partnership interest?

SECTION 2. ALLOCATION OF NONRECOURSE DEBT

1. Art contributed $10,000, and Beverly, Chuck, and Darlene each contributed $30,000 to the ABCD partnership, which then borrowed $900,000 to purchase a building for $1,000,000. The partners share all items of income and deduction in proportion to their respective capital contributions.

(a) The partnership is a general partnership and the loan is a recourse loan. What is each partner's basis in the partner's partnership interest?

(b) The partnership is a limited partnership, Art is the general partner and the others are limited partners, and the loan is a recourse loan. What is each partner's basis in the partner's partnership interest?

(c) The partnership is a general partnership and the loan is a nonrecourse loan secured by the building. What is each partner's basis in the partner's partnership interest?

(d) The partnership is a limited partnership, Art is the general partner and the others are limited partners, and the loan is a nonrecourse loan secured by the building. What is each partner's basis in the partner's partnership interest?

(e) What is the result in (d) if the debt is nonrecourse but Art, the sole general partner, personally guarantees the loan?

(f) What is the result in (d) if the debt is nonrecourse but Art, the sole general partner, personally guarantees up to $500,000 of the nonrecourse debt?

(g)(1) What is the result in (b) if Beverly, a limited partner, personally guarantees the recourse debt?

(2) What is the result in (d) if Beverly, a limited partner, personally guarantees the nonrecourse debt?

(h) What is the result in (d) if each partner personally guarantees a proportionate share of the nonrecourse debt?

2. Elvira and Fred formed a limited partnership in which Elvira is the general partner and Fred is the limited partner. Elvira contributed $10,000 for a 20 percent interest in partnership income and loss and Fred contributed $40,000 for an 80 percent interest in partnership income and loss. The partnership borrowed $850,000 pursuant to a nonrecourse loan and constructed an office building on leased land at a cost of $900,000. Interest on the loan is payable annually, but the principal is not due for 30 years. Assume that the cost recovery period for the building is 30 years; the method is straight-line. The partnership agreement contains all of the provisions necessary for allocations of deductions based on nonrecourse debt to be respected. The partnership's gross income exactly equals its deductible cash flow expenses, so each year the partnership reports a loss of $30,000 attributable to depreciation deductions.

What are Elvira's and Fred's respective shares of the nonrecourse debt, and their respective basis in their partnership interests:

(a) Immediately after the debt was incurred?

(b) At the end of the second year?

(c) At the end of the third year?

(d) At the end of 30 years?

3. Gloria and Hank are equal partners in the GH partnership. The partnership owns Whiteacre, which has a basis of $90,000 and a fair market value of $120,000. Whiteacre is subject to a nonrecourse mortgage of $108,000. Ira contributed $12,000 to become a one-half partner, and Gloria's and Hank's interests in profits and losses were reduced to one-quarter. In connection with Ira's admission to the partnership, the partnership revalued its assets and capital accounts for book purposes. What are the respective partner's shares of the nonrecourse debt and their bases in their partnership interests after Ira's admission to the partnership?

CHAPTER 6

TRANSACTIONS BETWEEN PARTNERS AND THE PARTNERSHIP

SECTION 1. TRANSACTIONS INVOLVING SERVICES, RENTS, AND LOANS

1. Alice and Bob are general partners in a real estate business. Alice is a two-thirds partner and Bob is a one-third partner. At the beginning of the year Alice's basis for her partnership interest was $10,000; Bob's basis for his partnership interest was $5,000. This year the AB partnership recognized taxable income of $9,000 from transactions with nonpartners. The partnership uses the accrual method of accounting and the partners use the cash method.

   (a)(1) What are the tax consequences to Alice and Bob if Bob is a lawyer and the partnership paid Bob $6,000 to defend a negligence suit against the partnership by a person who was injured in a "slip and fall" in a building owned by the partnership?

   (2) What would be the tax consequences to Alice and Bob if Bob billed the partnership for the services in the current year, but the partnership did not pay Bob until April of next year, in which the partnership again realized $9,000 of taxable income from transactions with unrelated parties?

   (b) Bob is a lawyer and the partnership paid Bob $6,000 to represent it in purchasing an apartment building (e.g., conduct the title search, etc). What are the tax consequences to Alice and Bob?

   (c) The partnership paid Bob $6,000 to serve as resident manager of one of its apartment buildings; the amount was unconditionally due if he rendered the services. What are the tax consequences to Alice and Bob?

   (d) Bob served as resident manager of one of the partnership's apartment buildings; the partnership agreed to pay Bob $6,000, but the payment was not made until April of the following year, in which the partnership again realized $9,000 of taxable income from transactions with unrelated parties. What are the tax consequences to Alice and Bob?

(e) What are the tax consequences to Alice and Bob if the partnership paid Bob $6,000 to oversee construction of a new apartment building being constructed for the partnership by an unrelated contracting company? Does it matter whether Bob holds himself out to third parties as engaged in a business providing the services that he provided to the partnership?

2. (a) Carla and Don are the members of a limited liability company that is taxed as a partnership and which operates a funeral home. Although they are equal members, because Don has assumed sole responsibility for responding to nighttime calls, the LLC provides Don with an apartment on the second floor of the funeral home. The LLC's expenses allocable to the apartment are $5,000, and the fair rental value of the apartment is $6,000. What are the tax consequences of this arrangement to Carla and Don?

   (b) Don and Carla's LLC paid all of the premiums for group health insurance benefits for its three employees, as well as for Carla and Don. The premium attributable to each person was $2,000. What are the tax results to Carla and Don?

3. Jackie and Kerry are general partners in an investment partnership. Jackie contributed $450,000 and Kerry contributed $200,000. They agreed that until Jackie had cumulatively withdrawn distributions totaling $250,000 more than Kerry had withdrawn, Jackie would receive annually, before dividing partnership profits, an amount equal to 6% of the excess of Jackie's capital account over Kerry's capital account. For the current year the partnership has net ordinary income of $12,000 and $8,000 of long-term capital gain. Because Jackie's capital account exceeded Kerry's by $250,000, Jackie was paid $15,000 as a guaranteed return on the excess capital contribution. What are the tax consequences to Jackie and Kerry?

4. Alito has been admitted as a new partner in the law firm of Scalia, Thomas & Roberts. Alito is entitled to 25 percent of the partnership's profits, but in the first year is guaranteed a minimum cash draw out of profits of $50,000. What are the tax consequences to Alito and the other partners if the partnership's profit in Alito's first year as a partner is $100,000? What if partnership profits are $200,000?

5. Andy is a civil engineer. Yosemite Development Associates, a general partnership, has offered Andy a 10 percent partnership interest, but with a zero opening capital account, if Andy will become the managing

partner of Yosemite for the next four years. The principal activity of Yosemite during that time will be the development and construction of an amusement park, which will be developed in several stages. In year 1 the expected profits will be zero; in year 2 the expected profits will be $1,000,000; in year 3 the expected profits will be $2,000,000; and in year 4 the expected profits will be $3,000,000. At the end of year 4 it is expected that Andy will receive a full distribution of the balance in Andy's capital account and Andy will cease to be a partner. How will the allocation of operating profits to Andy be treated under §§ 704 and § 707? Would your answer change if after year 4 Andy's capital account balance (if any) were not distributed, but Andy's continuing interest in the partnership profits was reduced to 1 percent?

SECTION 2. SALES OF PROPERTY

1. Andy, Bev, Cleo and Dean are partners in the ABCD Partnership. Andy has a 40 percent interest in profits and capital; Bev has a 30 percent interest; Cleo has a 20 percent interest; and Dean has a 10 percent interest. Andy sold Blackacre, an office building that had a basis of $120,000, to the partnership for $100,000. Two years later the partnership sold Blackacre. What are the tax consequences of the two transactions given the following additional facts:

   (a) Andy and Dean are siblings; the partners are otherwise unrelated. The partnership sold Blackacre for $80,000 to X Corp., which is equally owned by Andy and Andy's spouse.

   (b) Andy and Cleo are siblings; the partners are otherwise unrelated. The partnership sold Blackacre to an unrelated party for $150,000.

   (c) Andy and Cleo are siblings; the partners are otherwise unrelated. The partnership sold Blackacre to an unrelated party for $75,000.

   (d) The partners of ABCD are unrelated. The ABCD Partnership sold Blackacre for $75,000 to the CA Partnership, in which Cleo's spouse has a 90 percent interest in profits and capital and Andy's son's wholly owned corporation has a 10 percent interest.

   (e) The partners of ABCD are unrelated. The ABCD Partnership sold Blackacre for $75,000 to Bev's grandchild.

   (f) Andy and Cleo are siblings; the partners are otherwise unrelated. The partnership sold Blackacre to Cleo for $150,000.

2. (a) Ed and Fran are equal partners in the EF LLC, which holds investment assets and cash totaling $4,000,000. Ed's and Fran's bases

in their partnership interests are $1,750,000 each. On February 1st Ed contributed Whiteacre, which had a fair market value of $2,000,000 and an adjusted basis of $600,000, to the LLC, and Ed's capital account was increased by $2,000,000. On July 1st, the EF LLC distributed $1,500,000 in cash to Ed. Ed's capital account was reduced by $1,500,000. How should these transactions be treated for tax purposes?

(b) How should the transactions be treated for tax purposes if the distribution was received by Ed on August 1st three years later and was in the amount of $1,736,438?

3. (a) Gail and Harvey formed the GH Partnership (a general partnership). Gail contributed $400,000 of cash and has a one-third interest in profits and loss. Harvey contributed Greenacre, which had a fair market value of $2,000,000 and was subject to a $1,200,000 mortgage. Harvey's basis in Greenacre was $500,000. Harvey has a two-thirds interest in profits and loss. Harvey incurred the debt secured by the mortgage last year and used the proceeds to purchase publicly traded securities. What are the tax consequences of the transfer of Greenacre to the partnership?

   (b) What would be the consequences if Harvey had incurred the loan a year and a half ago to pay for environmental remediation costs (that were deductible under § 162) with respect to Greenacre?

   (c) What would be the result if Harvey incurred the loan three years ago to purchase publicly traded securities?

4. Memorial Hospital, a tax exempt organization, owns a building suitable for use as a medical laboratory. Memorial has formed an LLC with Ben and Casey, cash method individuals who operate a medical laboratory. Memorial has contributed the building and Ben and Casey have contributed a going medical laboratory business (previously conducted in leased premises) and cash. Memorial's capital account was credited with $1,000,000, but the fair market value of the building very likely was closer to $2,000,000. The LLC agreement allocates the first $200,000 of annual profits equally between Ben and Casey; all remaining profits are allocated to Memorial until Memorial has been allocated cumulative profits of $1,700,000. At that time, which the parties expect to be in about three years, Memorial will receive a liquidating distribution of the balance in Memorial's capital account and Memorial's LLC interest will terminate. How should this transaction be treated under §§ 704 and 707?

CHAPTER 7

SPECIAL LIMITATIONS ON LOSS DEDUCTIONS AT THE PARTNER LEVEL

SECTION 2. THE AT-RISK RULES OF SECTION 465

1. (a) Al is a general partner of a limited partnership formed last year to engage in oil and gas drilling and production. Al contributed $5,000 to obtain his interest in January of last year. The partnership borrowed funds on both a recourse basis and a nonrecourse basis to drill an oil well. Al's share of the recourse debt is $20,000, and his share of the nonrecourse debt is $100,000. The oil well produced some oil, but the revenue was less than the deductible expenses to drill and operate the oil well. Last year Al's distributive share of partnership income or loss was an operating loss of $40,000. The partnership made no distributions. How much of the $40,000 loss is deductible by Al after taking § 465 into account?

   (b) This year Al contributed an additional $10,000 to the partnership in connection with the partnership's acquisition of a herd of cattle to be raised on the portion of its ranch land not devoted to oil and gas production. To finance acquisition of the cattle, the partnership borrowed funds from a bank in which a limited partner owns 25 percent of the stock. Al's share of the recourse debt owed to the bank is $20,000, and his share of the nonrecourse debt owed to the bank is $90,000. Al's share of losses from the cattle ranching was $14,000. Al's share of profits from the oil and gas well, however, was $22,000. The partnership made no distributions. How much must Al include or may Al deduct on his return this year after taking § 465 into account?

2. Beth invested $50,000 in a limited liability company that is taxed as a partnership, which was formed to develop and market computer software. Beth obtained a one-fifth membership interest. The LLC borrowed $1,000,000 from an unrelated venture capital fund to commence its operations. Beth's share of the LLC's indebtedness was $200,000. Beth's distributive share of losses, which were largely attributable to § 174 deductions from the LLC for the first year, was

$200,000. How much of the $200,000 loss is deductible under the following circumstances:

(a) Each of the five equal members of the LLC guaranteed up to $100,000 of the loan.

(b) Beth personally guaranteed the entire $1,000,000 loan, and none of the other members of the LLC guaranteed the loan.

(c) All five of the equal members of the LLC personally guaranteed the entire $1,000,000 loan.

(d) The LLC agreement provides that each equal member will contribute up to an additional $75,000 to the LLC upon the vote of a majority of the interests in the LLC, which is member managed LLC.

3. (a) Calvin contributed $100,000 to become a limited partner with a one-tenth interest in a limited partnership formed to purchase Blackacre, a high rise apartment building. The partnership paid $10 million for Blackacre, the portion of the purchase price in excess of the partners' contributions being obtained through a $9,000,000 nonrecourse loan from the Last National Bank. Calvin's share of the debt was $900,000. In each of the first five years of the partnership, Calvin's distributive share of partnership income or loss was a $35,000 loss. To what extent do the at-risk rules limit the amount that Calvin may deduct?

   (b) To what extent do the at-risk rules limit the amount that Calvin may deduct if 60 percent of the stock in the Last National Bank is owned by the spouse of the general partner?

   (c) To what extent do the at-risk rules limit the amount that Calvin may deduct if instead of borrowing $9,000,000 from the Last National Bank the partnership gave the seller of Blackacre $1,000,000 in cash and a $9,000,000 nonrecourse promissory note, secured by the property and on commercially reasonable terms?

SECTION 3. THE PASSIVE ACTIVITY LOSS RULES OF SECTION 469

1. Jane is an actress who is a 10 percent partner in the Macon Braves, a minor league baseball team. The Macon Braves partnership had a net loss in the current year. Jane's basis in her partnership interest, prior to taking into account this year's loss, is $150,000.

(a) Jane is a limited partner. She performed no services for the Macon Braves Her distributive share from the Macon Braves was a $60,000 loss. She earned $2,000,000 from acting this year. May she deduct her distributive share of Macon Braves' losses against her acting income?

(b) Jane is a general partner. She performed no services for the Macon Braves. Her distributive share from the Macon Braves was a $60,000 loss. She earned $2,000,000 from acting this year. May she deduct her distributive share of Macon Braves' losses against her acting income?

(c) Jane is a general partner. She took a hiatus in her acting career and served as the team's general manager, for which she received a guaranteed payment of $40,000. Her distributive share from the Macon Braves was a $60,000 loss. She received $200,000 of interest and dividends on publicly traded securities this year. May she deduct her distributive share of Macon Braves' losses against her guaranteed payment and her interest and dividend income?

(d) Jane is a general partner, but the only service she performed for the partnership was to "star" in three filmed television commercials, for which she received a guaranteed payment of $10,000. Her distributive share from the Macon Braves was a $60,000 loss. She received $1,000,000 from acting this year. May she deduct her distributive share of Macon Braves' losses against her guaranteed payment and acting income?

(e) Jane is a limited partner. She performed no services for the Macon Braves Her distributive share from the Macon Braves was a $60,000 loss; that loss consisted of $5,000 of interest income on the working capital of the Macon Braves and a $65,000 loss from other items. She earned $2,000,000 from acting this year. What are the tax consequences to Jane?

(f) What would be the result in (a) if Jane also realized $45,000 of net income from a real estate limited partnership interest in which she has invested as a limited partner?

(g) What would be the result in question (b) if the Macon Braves operated through an LLC classified as a partnership? Does it matter whether the LLC is member managed or manager managed and, if it is manager managed, whether Jane is an LLC manager?

2. Jerry and Kathy formed the JK Partnership for purposes of purchasing and leasing an office building. Each partner contributed $500,000 for a one-half partnership interest. The partnership borrowed $9,000,000 and purchased a building for $10,000,000. For the current year the partnership realized an operating loss of $200,000; each partner's

distributive share of the loss was $100,000. Jerry is engaged primarily in the construction business, from which his annual income is $250,000; Kathy is a physician and earns $300,000 annually.

(a) Jerry serves as managing partner and leasing agent for the building. Kathy performs no services for the partnership. May either Jerry or Kathy deduct his or her share of partnership losses against his or her other income?

(b) Kathy serves as managing partner and leasing agent for the building. Jerry performs no services for the partnership. May either Jerry or Kathy deduct his or her share of partnership losses against his or her other income?

3. Emma is an investment banker, who earns $500,000 per year. She is a limited partner in Derby Associates, a thoroughbred horse breeding partnership in which she does not materially participate. Her basis in the partnership is $100,000, which is attributable to a $25,000 cash contribution, $30,000 of partnership recourse debt, and $45,000 of partnership nonrecourse debt. Her distributive share of partnership losses for the year was $70,000. Emma also is a limited partner in Petro Associates, which produces oil. Her distributive share from Petro Associates is a profit of $8,000. Assuming that Emma has no other relevant items, what is Emma's adjusted gross income for the year?

CHAPTER 8

SALES OF PARTNERSHIP INTERESTS BY PARTNERS

SECTION 1. THE SELLER'S SIDE OF THE TRANSACTION

1. Blake is a general partner in the BCD limited partnership; Charlie and Dave are limited partners. Blake's interest is 20 percent and Charlie's and Dave's interests are each 40 percent. The basis of Blake's general partnership interest is $200 and its fair market value is $300. Each of Charlie and Dave has a $400 basis in their partnership interests, which are worth $600. The partnership has no debts and distributes all of its taxable income currently.

   (a) Blake buys one-half of Charlie's limited partnership interest for $300. What are the tax consequences to Charlie?

   (b) Blake buys all of Charlie's limited partnership interest for $600, following which Blake sells all of the general partnership interest to Dave for $300. What are the tax consequences to Blake?

   (c) Blake buys all of Charlie's limited partnership interest for $600, following which Blake sells all of the limited partnership interest to Elvis for $600. What are the tax consequences to Blake?

2. Ernesto and Fran are general partners in the EF partnership. Ernesto contributed $1,000 for his one-third partnership interest in profits and loss. Fran contributed $2,000 for a two-thirds partnership interest in profits and loss. The partnership borrowed $1,200 to invest in marketable securities, which it purchased for $4,200. When the partnership assets had appreciated to $4,800, Ernesto sold one-half of his general partnership interest to Gary for $600 cash. What is the tax consequence to Ernesto of the sale?

3. Ken owns a one-third interest in the KLM Partnership, which develops real estate. The partnership both constructs real estate for sale to customers and holds real estate for rental purposes.

   (a) KLM uses the cash method of accounting. The assets and partners' capital accounts of the KLM Partnership are as follows:

Asset	Adjusted Basis	F.M.V.	Capital Accounts	Adjusted Basis	F.M.V.
Cash	$ 45,000	$ 45,000	K	$110,000	$180,000
Accounts Receivable	0	$ 60,000	L	$110,000	$180,000
Store Building (for sale)	$150,000	$180,000	M	$110,000	$180,000
Office Building (for rent)	$135,000	$240,000			
Goodwill, etc.	0	$ 15,000			
	$330,000	$540,000		$330,000	$540,000

What are the tax consequences to Ken if, on January 1st, Ken sells his partnership interest to Niki for $180,000 in cash?

(b) KLM uses the cash method of accounting. The assets and partners capital accounts of the KLM Partnership are as follows:

Assets	Adjusted Basis	F.M.V.	Capital Accounts	Adjusted Basis	F.M.V.
Cash	$ 45,000	$ 45,000	K	$190,000	$180,000
Accounts Receivable	$ 0	$ 60,000	L	$190,000	$180,000
Store Building (for sale)	$150,000	$180,000	M	$190,000	$180,000
Office Building (for rent)	$375,000	$240,000			
Goodwill, etc.	$ 0	$ 15,000			
	$570,000	$540,000		$570,000	$540,000

What are the tax consequences to Ken if, on January 1st, Ken sells his partnership interest to Niki for $180,000 in cash?

(c) KLM use the accrual method of accounting. The assets and partners' capital accounts of the KLM Partnership are as follows:

Assets	Adjusted Basis	F.M.V.	Capital Accounts	Adjusted Basis	F.M.V.
Cash	$ 45,000	$ 45,000	K	$130,000	$180,000
Accounts Receivable	$ 60,000	$ 60,000	L	$130,000	$180,000
Store Building (for sale)	$150,000	$180,000	M	$130,000	$180,000
Office Building (for rent)	$135,000	$240,000			
Goodwill, etc.	$ 0	$ 15,000			
	$390,000	$540,000		$390,000	$540,000

What are the tax consequences to Ken if on January 1st, Ken sells his partnership interest to Niki for $180,000 in cash?

4. Oliver and Pam are equal members in the OP LLC. The LLC has a concession to operate a marina on a lake in a national park. The OP LLC uses the accrual method of accounting. The marina is very profitable, and each member earns and withdraws over $100,000 annually. The assets that the LLC carries on its books are as follows:

Asset	Adjusted Basis	F.M.V.
Cash	$ 50,000	$ 50,000
Inventory	$ 40,000	$ 50,000
Marina	$250,000	$500,000
Rental Boats	$ 60,000	$100,000

All of the gain inherent in the rental boats is § 1245 gain; none of the gain inherent in the marina is § 1245 gain. Pam's basis for her interest in the OP LLC is $200,000. Pam sold her interest in the OP LLC to Quinn for $600,000 in cash, which is $250,000 more than the fair market value of one-half of the tangible assets. How much of Pam's gain is ordinary income under § 751? Does it matter how the intangible assets of the OP LLC are characterized, e.g., goodwill versus concession rights?

5. Ralph and Sandy are equal general partners in a funeral home business. The RS Partnership reports income from sales of caskets on the accrual method and income from services on the cash method. The assets of the RS Partnership, including goodwill, are as follows:

Asset	Adjusted Basis	F.M.V.
Cash	$ 20,000	$ 20,000
Accounts Receivable	$ 20,000	$ 50,000
Inventory	$ 50,000	$ 70,000
Funeral Home	$150,000	$200,000
Equipment	$ 60,000	$100,000
Goodwill	$ 0	$ 60,000

All of the gain inherent in the equipment is § 1245 gain; none of the gain inherent in the funeral home is § 1245 gain. Ralph's basis for his interest in the RS Partnership is $150,000. Ralph sold his interest in the partnership to Sandy for $520,000, of which $130,000 was payable at the closing. The remaining $390,000, with adequate interest, was due two years later. To what extent may Ralph report the sale using the § 453 installment method?

SECTION 2. THE PURCHASER'S SIDE OF THE TRANSACTION: BASIS ASPECTS

1. Alex and Bernie are equal general partners in a plumbing business. The AB Partnership reports income from sales of inventory on the accrual method and income from services on the cash method. The assets of the AB Partnership, including goodwill, are as follows:

Asset	Adjusted Basis And Book Value	F.M.V.
Cash	$ 10,000	$ 10,000
Accounts Receivable	$ 20,000	$ 50,000
Inventory	$ 50,000	$ 80,000
Equipment	$ 80,000	$130,000
Goodwill	$ 0	$ 60,000
	$160,000	$330,000

The AB Partnership owes a bank $30,000 on a purchase money loan to acquire some of the equipment and $2,000 to trade creditors for bills that it properly accounts for on the cash method. Cliff purchased Alex's partnership interest for a cash payment of $150,000. The "new" BC partnership promised to indemnify Alex on the debts to the bank.

(a) What is Cliff's basis in his partnership interest?

(b) Should Cliff request that a § 754 election be made? Why? Compare the effects on Cliff of subsequent normal partnership operations assuming, alternatively, that an election has been made and that one has not been made.

(c) Are there any reasons why Bernie might hesitate to agree to a § 754 election?

2. Donna purchased Dennis' one-third interest of the DEF LLC (which is taxed as a partnership) for $125,000. In connection with Dona's purchase, the LLC made a § 754 election. The DEF LLC uses the accrual method of accounting with respect to sales of inventory and the cash method with respect to the provision of services. When Donna purchased her one-third interest, the DEF LLC's assets and capital accounts (which were revalued at F.M.V.) were as follows:

Assets	Adjusted Basis	F.M.V.	Capital Accounts	Adjusted Basis	F.M.V.
Cash	$ 9,000	$ 9,000	D	$ 75,000	$125,000
Accounts Receivable	$ 6,000	$ 36,000	E	$ 75,000	$125,000
Inventory	$ 60,000	$120,000	F	$ 75,000	$125,000
Land	$ 45,000	$ 30,000			
Building	$105,000	$180,000			
	$225,000	$375,000		$225,000	$375,000

The land and building are § 1231 assets.

Determine the § 743(b) special basis for each of the LLC's assets with respect to Donna.

3. Erin purchased Fritz's one-third interest in The Big Short Partnership for $100,000. The partnership, which is a dealer in securities, holds most of its securities as inventory, but some are held as capital assets. Its security holdings at the time Erin purchased her interest were as follows:

Asset	Adjusted Basis	F.M.V.
Inventory	$165,000	$240,000
Capital Assets	$135,000	$ 60,000

Would Erin have benefited from a § 754 election made in connection with her purchase of the partnership interest?

4. Glenda and Hector are partners in the GH partnership which owns a commercial office building. The fair market value of the building is $600,000, its basis is $1,000,000. The building is subject to a mortgage of $500,000. The basis of each of Glenda's and Hector's partnership interest is $500,000. Hector sells his partnership interest to Inez for $50,000. The partnership does not make a § 754 election. Does the absence of the election make a difference?

CHAPTER 9

PARTNERSHIP DISTRIBUTIONS

SECTION 1. CURRENT DISTRIBUTIONS

A. CASH DISTRIBUTIONS AND REDUCTION OF LIABILITIES

B. PROPERTY DISTRIBUTIONS

1. Amy and Blair are equal partners in a law practice. At the beginning of the year the basis of Amy's partnership interest was $3,000 and the basis of Blair's partnership interest was $5,000. On the last day of each month during the taxable year, Amy and Blair each withdrew $600 out of current cash flow. At the close of the year it was determined that each partner's distributive share of partnership profits was $4,000. What are the tax consequences to Amy and Blair?

2. Connie, Dallas, and Eddie are partners in the CDE partnership. For the current year, the partnership expects to realize no taxable income. The assets and partners' capital accounts of the CDE Partnership are as follows:

Partnership Assets				Partners' Capital			
Asset	Book Value	Basis	FMV		Book Value	Basis	FMV
Cash	$360	$360	$360	Connie	$293	$425	$400
Mauveacre	$110	$110	$190	Dallas	$220	$210	$300
Whiteacre	$ 20	$ 20	$100	Eddie	$147	$ 25	$200
Blackacre	$140	$140	$100				
Greenacre	$ 20	$ 20	$ 80				
Brownacre	$ 10	$ 10	$ 70				
	$660	$660	$900		$660	$660	$900

All of the properties owned by the partnership are § 1231 assets.

To reduce Eddie's interest from two-ninths to one-eighth, the partnership plans to distribute $100 worth of property to him on July 1st. What would be the tax consequences of the following alternatives?

(a) The partnership distributes Whiteacre to Eddie.

(b) The partnership distributes Blackacre to Eddie.

(c) The partnership distributes $20 cash and Greenacre to Eddie.

(d) The partnership distributes $30 of cash and Brownacre to Eddie.

3. Regan is a partner in Yosemite Acres Real Estate Development Associates. The basis of Regan's partnership interest is $9,000. The partnership holds various parcels of real estate, some of which are held for sale to customers in the ordinary course of business and some of which are held for rental. To reduce its holdings, the partnership distributed to each partner, in proportion to the partner's capital interest in the partnership, undivided interests in Blackacre and Whiteacre. The fair market value of the interest in Blackacre received by Regan was $7,500 and the portion of the partnership's basis for the interest in Blackacre received by Regan was $12,000. The fair market value of the interest in Whiteacre received by Regan was $15,000 and the portion of the partnership's basis for the interest in Whiteacre received by Regan was $6,000. What is Regan's basis in Whiteacre and Blackacre if:

   (a) Whiteacre was held for sale to customers in the ordinary course of business and Blackacre was held for rental?

   (b) Blackacre was held for sale to customers in the ordinary course of business and Whiteacre was held for rental?

   (c) Both properties were:

      (1) held for sale to customers in the ordinary course of business?

      (2) held for rental?

4. Gene and Helen, cash method individuals, are equal partners in the AB Partnership. The assets and liabilities of the partnership are as follows:

Assets	Adjusted Basis/Book Value	F.M.V.	Liabilities & Partners' Capital	Basis	Book Value	F.M.V
Cash	$60,000	$ 60,000	Blackacre mortgage		$ 90,000	
Blackacre	$30,000	$150,000				
Whiteacre	$80,000	$120,000	Whiteacre mortgage		$ 60,000	
			Gene	$ 85,000	$ 10,000	$ 90,000
			Helen	$ 85,000	$ 10,000	$ 90,000
	$170,000	$330,000		$170,000	$170,000	$180,000

The adjusted basis of the partnership's assets equals their book value. Blackacre and Whiteacre are both § 1231 assets. To reduce Gene's interest in the partnership to a one-quarter interest, the partnership distributed Whiteacre to Gene subject to the mortgage, which Gene assumed. Both Gene and Helen had an $85,000 basis in their respective partnership interests before the distribution. What are the tax consequences to Gene and Helen?

C. DISTRIBUTIONS BY PARTNERSHIPS HOLDING UNREALIZED RECEIVABLES OR SUBSTANTIALLY APPRECIATED INVENTORY

1. The LMN Partnership' assets and partner's capital accounts are as follows:

Assets	Adjusted Basis/ Book Value	F.M.V.	Partners' Capital	Adjusted Basis/ Book Value	F.M.V.
Cash	$120,000	$120,000	L	$105,000	$150,000
Inventory	$ 75,000	$150,000	M	$105,000	$150,000
Blackacre	$ 60,000	$ 75,000	N	$105,000	$150,000
Whiteacre	$ 60,000	$105,000			
	$315,000	$450,000		$315,000	$450,000

Blackacre and Whiteacre are both § 1231 property.

(a) The partnership distributes $75,000 of cash to L. As a result of the distribution L's interest is reduced from a one-third to a one-fifth interest in the partnership, worth $75,000, after the distribution. What are the consequences to L and the partnership (including M's and N's distributive share of any income items) as a result of the distribution?

(b) The partnership distributes Blackacre to L to reduce L's interest to one-fifth. What are the consequences to L and the partnership (including M's and N's distributive share of any income items) as a result of the distribution?

(c) The partnership distributes one-half of the inventory to L to reduce L's interest to one-fifth. What are the consequences to L and the partnership (including M's and N's distributive share of any income items) as a result of the distribution?

SECTION 2. "MIXING BOWL" TRANSACTIONS: DISTRIBUTIONS OF CONTRIBUTED PROPERTY

1. X Corporation and Y Corporation formed the XY LLC on July 1, 2010. X Corporation contributed Blackacre, which was § 1231 rental property with a basis of $5,000,000 and a fair market value of $12,000,000. Y Corporation contributed $12,000,000 in cash. X Corporation and Y Corporation shared profits and losses as follows: Y Corporation was allocated the first $1,000,000 of gross income, all of the depreciation, and the first $200,000 of expenses all with respect to Blackacre; X Corporation was allocated the first $900,000 of income resulting from investing the $12,000,000 in cash in investment grade stocks and securities; after these preliminary allocations, X Corporation and Y Corporation split profits and losses equally.

   (a) On June 30, 2017, the XY LLC distributes Blackacre to Y Corporation. At that time, the basis of Blackacre was $4,500,000; its fair market value was $14,000,000. Immediately before the distribution, Y Corporation's basis in its interest in the LLC was $15,000,000 and its capital account also was $15,000,000; X Corporation's basis in its interest in the LLC was $9,000,000 and its capital account was $15,000,000. What are the tax consequences of the distribution to both X Corporation and Y Corporation?

   (b) How would your answer differ if the distribution of Blackacre to Y Corporation occurred on July 1, 2017 (assuming that all of the values and bases remained unchanged?

2. The basic facts are the same as in problem 1.

   (a) On June 30, 2017, the XY LLC distributes $14,000,000 to X Corporation. At that time, the basis of Blackacre was $4,500,000; its fair market value was $14,000,000. Immediately before the distribution, Y Corporation's basis in its interest in the LLC was $16,000,000 and its capital account also was $16,000,000; X Corporation's basis in its interest in the LLC was $10,000,000 and its capital account was $16,000,000. What are the tax consequences of the distribution to both X Corporation and Y Corporation?

(b) How would your answer differ if the distribution of $14,000,000 to X Corporation occurred on July 1, 2017 (assuming that all of the values and bases remained unchanged?

SECTION 3. DISTRIBUTIONS IN LIQUIDATION OF A PARTNER'S INTEREST

A. 736(b) PAYMENTS

1. The ABC Partnership conducts a retail lumber and hardware business. It has the following assets and partners' capital accounts restated to reflect fair market values:

Assets	Adjusted Basis\ Book Value	F.M.V.	Partners' Capital	Adjusted Basis/ Book Value	F.M.V/
Cash	$165,000	$165,000	A	$244,000	$235,000
Lumber Inventory	$150,000	$120,000	B	$244,000	$235,000
			C	$244,000	$235,000
Hardware Inventory	$100,000	$114,000			
Blackacre	$120,000	$150,000			
Whiteacre	$197,000	$111,000			
Goodwill	$ 0	$ 45,000			
	$732,000	$705,000		$732,000	$705,000

Blackacre and Whiteacre are § 1231 assets. The partnership is planning to make a liquidating distribution to C and is considering several alternatives. What are the tax consequences of each of the following alternative liquidating distributions?

(a) C receives Blackacre and $85,000 of cash in complete liquidation of C's interest in the partnership.

(b) C receives the Lumber Inventory and $115,000 of cash in complete liquidation of C's interest in the partnership.

(c) C receives the Hardware Inventory and $121,000 of cash in complete liquidation of C's interest in the partnership.

2. The DEF LLC conducts retail men's and women's clothing businesses. It has the following assets, liabilities, and members' capital accounts:

Partnership Capital

Assets	Adjusted Basis	Book Value	F.M.V.
Cash	$255,000	$255,000	$255,000
Men's Inventory	$ 15,000	$ 15,000	$ 90,000
Women's Inventory	$ 90,000	$ 90,000	$180,000
Blackacre	$150,000	$150,000	$180,000
Whiteacre	$135,000	$135,000	$105,000
Goodwill	$ 0	$ 0	$ 45,000
	$645,000	$645,000	$855,000

Partners' Adjusted Basis and Capital

	Adjusted Basis	Book Value	F.M.V.
Loan		$120,000	
D	$215,000	$175,000	$245,000
E	$215,000	$175,000	$245,000
F	$215,000	$175,000	$245,000
	$645,000	$645,000	$735,000

Blackacre and Whiteacre are § 1231 assets. The partnership is planning to make a liquidating distribution to F and is considering several alternatives. The basis of F's partnership interest is $215,000. What are the tax consequences of each of the following alternative liquidating distributions?

(a) F receives the Men's Clothing Inventory and $155,000 in cash.

(b) F receives the Men's Clothing Inventory, Whiteacre, and $50,000 in cash.

(c) F receives $245,000 in cash.

(d) F receives Blackacre and $65,000 in Cash.

(e) F receives the Woman's Clothing Inventory and $65,000 in cash.

B. 736(a) PAYMENTS

1. Jean owns a one-fourth interest in the profits and capital of the GHIJ Partnership. The GHIJ partnership is a cash method taxpayer and has conducted a travel agency business that the partnership purchased seven years ago. The partnership has the following assets and partners' capital accounts:

Assets	Adjusted Basis/ Book Value	F.M.V.	Partners' Capital	Adjusted Basis/ Book Value	F.M.V.
Cash	$36,000	$ 36,000	G	$16,000	$ 27,000
Accounts Receivable	$ 0	$ 12,000	H	$16,000	$ 27,000
Office Equipment	$20,000	$ 20,000	I	$16,000	$ 27,000
Goodwill	$ 8,000	$ 40,000	J	$16,000	$ 27,000
	$64,000	$108,000		$64,000	$108,000

Jean is planning to retire. Her basis for her partnership interest is $16,000. The partnership agreement has no express provisions regarding payments to a retiring partner.

(a) What are the tax consequences to Jean and to the partnership (i.e., the remaining partners) if the partnership distributes $27,000 in cash to Jean in complete liquidation of her partnership interest?

(b)(1) Could the result in (a) be changed by amending the partnership agreement in conjunction with Jean's retirement to provide that a retiring partner would be paid for the partner's share of the partnership's goodwill? If so, is it more likely that Jean or the continuing partners would suggest such an amendment?

(2) What would be the result if the partnership agreement is amended as provided in (b)(1), but Jean is paid $30,000 in cash?

(c) What are the tax consequences to Jean and to the partnership (i.e., the remaining partners) if the partnership agreement has no express provisions regarding payments to a retiring partner and the partnership distributes $10,000 to Jean immediately upon her withdrawal and an additional $10,000 in each of the next two years?

(d) What would be the result in (c) if instead of fixed payments, Jean received $10,000 immediately upon her withdrawal and one-eighth of each year's profits in each of the next two years and partnership profits were $80,000 per year, resulting in two $10,000 payments to Jean?

SECTION 4. BASIS ADJUSTMENTS TO REMAINING PARTNERSHIP ASSETS

1. The ABC Partnership had three equal partners, Al, Bette, and Claude. It had the following assets and partners' capital accounts:

Assets	Adjusted Basis/ Book Value	F.M.V.	Partners' Capital	Adjusted Basis/ Book Value	F.M.V.
Cash	$ 40,000	$ 40,000	Al	$ 60,000	$ 90,000
Blackacre	$ 90,000	$ 45,000	Bette	$ 60,000	$ 90,000
Whiteacre	$ 10,000	$ 55,000	Claude	$ 60,000	$ 90,000
Greenacre	$ 40,000	$130,000			
	$180,000	$270,000		$180,000	$270,000

All of the assets are § 1231 assets. In the current year, Claude received Blackacre in a disproportionate nonliquidating distribution. As a result of the distribution, Claude thereafter had a one-fifth interest in partnership capital and profits worth $50,000. Assuming that the partnership has not already made a § 754 election, should it make a § § 754 election in connection with the distribution to Claude?

2. Don, Eve, and Fay are partners in the DEF Partnership, which is engaged in real estate investment and development. The partnership holds some subdivision lots for sale and two properties, Blackacre and Whiteacre, for rental purposes. The DEF Partnership had the following assets and partners' capital accounts:

Assets	Adjusted Basis/ Book Value	F.M.V.	Partners' Capital	Adjusted Basis/ Book Value	F.M.V.
Cash	$ 30,000	$ 30,000	Don	$ 40,000	$ 60,000
Lots held for sale	$ 50,000	$ 60,000	Eve	$ 40,000	$ 60,000
			Fay	$ 40,000	$ 60,000
Blackacre	$ 10,000	$ 60,000			
Whiteacre	$ 30,000	$ 30,000			
	$120,000	$180,000		$120,000	$180,000

The partnership distributed Blackacre to Don in complete liquidation of his interest in the partnership. Should the partnership make a § 754 election in connection with the distribution?

3. Gina, Hank, and Ike are partners in the GHI Partnership, which is engaged in real estate investment and development. The partnership holds some subdivision lots for sale and three properties, Blackacre,

Greenacre, and Whiteacre, for rental purposes. The GHI Partnership had the following assets and partners' capital accounts:

Assets	Adjusted Basis/ Book Value	F.M.V.	Partners' Capital	Adjusted Basis/ Book Value	F.M.V.
Lots	$ 50,000	$ 60,000	Gina	$ 40,000	$ 60,000
Blackacre	$ 5,000	$ 60,000	Hank	$ 40,000	$ 60,000
Greenacre	$ 20,000	$ 30,000	Ike	$ 40,000	$ 60,000
Whiteacre	$ 45,000	$ 30,000			
	$120,000	$180,000		$120,000	$180,000

The three parcels of land are capital assets to the partnership. Gina receives Blackacre as a distribution in liquidation of her interest in the partnership.

(a) Disregarding § 736(a) and § 751, which are inapplicable under the facts, what are the tax consequences to Gina and to the partnership if there is no § 754 election in effect.

(b) What would be the result in (a) if the partnership made a § 754 election?

SECTION 5. SALE OF INTEREST TO OTHER PARTNERS VERSUS DISTRIBUTION

1. Arnie is a one-third limited partner in a real estate partnership. Each of the three partners contributed $450,000 in cash, although each partner is liable for an additional contribution of $450,000 if called for by the general partner. The partnership borrowed $9,000,000 from the Roulette Savings & Loan Association on a nonrecourse mortgage and purchased a shopping mall for $10,350,000. Cumulatively, Arnie's distributive share of profit and loss during the life of the partnership has been $1.8 million of losses. The partnership has conducted no other business, made no distributions, made no principal payments on its loan, and has no other assets. Arnie's basis in the partnership interest is $1,650,000; Arnie's capital account is negative $1,350,000. The general partner has called for each limited partner to contribute an additional $450,000 to be used for improvements to the property. Arnie does not want to contribute more than an additional $150,000, and is willing to reduce his interest in partnership profits and losses to one-ninth if the partnership will accept this lesser contribution. To accommodate Arnie's desires, Dale, who is not now a partner, will contribute $300,000 to the partnership and become a two-ninths partner. Is this transaction a sale of two-thirds of Arnie's partnership

interest to Dale or is it a distribution to Arnie coupled with the admission of Dale as a new partner? What difference does it make?

SECTION 6. COMPLETE LIQUIDATION OF THE PARTNERSHIP

1. Alex and Bev are partners in the AB Partnership. Alex is a two-thirds partner; Bev is a one-third partner. The assets and partners' capital accounts of the AB Partnership are as follows:

Partnership Capital

Assets	Adjusted Basis	Book	F.M.V.
Cash	$ 45,000	$ 45,000	$ 45,000
Accounts Receivable	0	0	$ 60,000
Store Building (for sale)	$150,000	$150,000	$180,000
Office Building (for rent)	$135,000	$135,000	$240,000
Goodwill, etc.	0	0	$ 15,000
	$330,000	$330,000	$540,000

Partners' Capital and Liabilities

	Adjusted Basis	Book	F.M.V.
Bank Loan		$30,000	
Alex	$220,000	$200,000	$340,000
Bev	$110,000	$100,000	$170,000
	$330,000	$330,000	$510,000

Alex paid Bev $170,000 in cash to purchase Bev's partnership interest. What are the tax consequences to the parties? How much income will Alex recognize on collection of the accounts receivable? How much gain would Alex recognize if she sold the Store Building for $190,000 one month later? How will Alex compute depreciation on the office building? Does it matter whether the AB Partnership had a § 754 election in effect?

2. Charlie, Dean, and Evan are one-third partners in the CDE partnership, which is engaged in real estate investment and development. The partnership holds some subdivision lots for sale and

two properties, Blackacre and Whiteacre, for rental purposes. The CDE Partnership had the following assets and partners' capital accounts:

Assets	Adjusted Basis/ Book Value	F.M.V.	Adjusted Partners' Capital	Basis/ Book Value	F.M.V.
Cash	$ 60,000	$ 60,000	Charlie	$30,000	$ 60,000
Lots held for sale	$21,000	$ 60,000	Dean	$30,000	$ 60,000
Blackacre	$ 9,000	$ 60,000	Evan	$30,000	$ 60,000
	$90,000	$180,000		$90,000	$180,000

Blackacre is a § 1231 asset that is not subject to § 1245 recapture.

The partnership liquidated by distributing the cash to Charlie, the lots to Dean and Blackacre to Evan. What are the tax consequences to the partners?

How would your answer differ if the partnership did not own and distribute Blackacre to Evan but instead owned and distributed to Evan a bulldozer (which originally cost the partnership $75,000) with an adjusted basis of $9,000 and a fair market value of $60,000?

3. Fran, Gene, and Hector were partners in the FGH partnership. The assets and partners' capital accounts of the FGH Partnership were as follows:

Assets	Adjusted Basis/ Book Value	F.M.V.	Liabilities & Partners' Capital	Adjusted Basis/ Book Value	F.M.V
Greenacre	$460	$ 360	Fran	$450	$ 400
Whiteacre	$120	$ 190	Gene	$150	$ 400
Blackacre	$ 70	$ 450	Hector	$ 50	$ 200
	$650	$1,000		$650	$1,000

All of the properties are § 1231 assets. The FGH partnership was a cash method, calendar year taxpayer.

(a) On July 1st of last year, Fran sold her partnership interest to Ike. On June 30th of this year, Hector sold his partnership interest to Jane. What are the tax consequences to Gene and Ike resulting from Hector's sale of his partnership interest to Jane?

(b) After Hector sold his interest to Jane, could the GIJ Partnership adopt the accrual method of accounting without first obtaining the

Commissioner's consent? Could the GHI partnership have done so after Fran sold her interest to Ike?

(c) Assuming that more than 40 percent of the gross receipts of the GIJ partnership are received in January and February, after Hector sold his interest to Jane, could the GIJ Partnership adopt a March 1 - February 28 fiscal year without first obtaining the Commissioner's consent? Could the GHI partnership have done so after Fran sold her interest to Ike?

(d) If in connection with the sale of Fran's partnership interest to Ike the partnership had made a § 754 election, would a new § 754 election be necessary in connection with the sale of Hector's interest to Jane in order to provide Jane with a § 743(b) basis adjustment?

SECTION 7. PARTNERSHIP MERGERS AND DIVISIONS

1. Ann and Bob were the members of the AB LLC, which had assets with a value of $600,000. Each had a one-half interest. Carla, Donnie, and Erin were the members of the CDE LLC, which had assets with a fair market value of $900,000. Each had a one-third interest.

(a) The AB LLC transferred all of its assets to the CDE LLC. Ann and Bob each received a one fifth interest in the CDE LLC and the interests of Carla, Donnie, and Erin were reduced to one-fifth each. The CDE LLC was renamed the ABCDE LLC

(1) Is the ABCDE LLC a new partnership, with each of the AB LLC and the CDE liquidating or is the ABCDE LLC a continuation of either the AB or CDE LLC?

(2) Would your answer differ if the AB LLC had assets worth $1,800,000 and Ann and Bob each acquired a one-third interest in the CDE LLC, which was renamed the ABCDE LLC, and Carla, Donnie, and Erin's interests were each reduced to one-ninth?

(3) Would your answer differ if the AB LLC had assets woRth $900,000 and Ann and Bob each acquired a one-fourth interest in the CDE LLC, which was renamed the ABCDE LLC, and Carla, Donnie, and Erin's interests were each reduced to one-sixth?

(b) Would your answers to Part a. differ if the combination of the two LLCs had been effected under a state statute providing for the merger of the two LLCs by operation of law?

(c) Would your answers to Part a. differ if the combination of the two LLCs hAd been effected by Ann and Bob transferring their interests in the AB LLC to the CDE LLC, in exchange for interests in the CDE LLC (renamed the ABCDE LLC, with the AB LLC continuing to exist unDer state law as wholly owned by the ABCDE LLC?

2. The members of the FGHIJ LLC were Fran, George, Helen, Ike, and Jean. The assets of the FGHIJ LLC were worth $1,000,000 and each member held a one-fifth interest.

(a) The FGHIJ LLC did vided by transferring $400,000 of assets to the newly formed FG LLC, which momentarily was wholly owned by the FGHIJ LLC, and immediately distributing a one-half interest in the FG LLC to each of Fran and George in complete liquidation of the their interests in the FGHIJ LLC, immediately after which the FGHIJ LLC was renamed the HIJ LLC. Which, if any of the FG LLC and the HIJ LLC is a continuing partnership and which, if any, is a newly formed partnership?

(b) Would your answer differ if as part of the transaction described in Part a. the interest of H was liquidated for $200,000 of cash and only IJ remained as members of the original LLC, which was renamed the IJ LLC?

SECTION 8. SPECIAL PROBLEMS ON THE LIQUIDATION OF A PARTNERSHIP INTEREST FOLLOWING THE DEATH OF A PARTNER

1. Art was a 20 percent partner in the AX Partnership. X Corporation was the only other partner. Because X Corporation reported on a fiscal year ending January 31st, the AX Partnership reported on a January 31st fiscal year. For the fiscal year that ended in January of this year, Art's distributive share of partnership income was $50,000. Art died on December 31st of this year, and his estate succeeded to his interest as a partner. For the fiscal year ending on January 31st of next year, the AX Partnership recognized $300,000 of income, of which $60,000 was allocable to Art and/or Art's estate. How much partnership income is reportable on the joint return filed by Art's surviving spouse for this year, and how much partnership income is reportable by Art's estate?

2. Juan, Karen, and Leo were members of the JKL LLC, which is taxed as a partnership. Each of them has a one-third interest. The LLC uses the cash method of accounting. Karen died last year and her estate succeeded to her interest as a member. At the time of Karen's death, the assets and capital accounts of the JKL LLC were as follows:

Assets	Adjusted Basis	F.M.V.	Capital Accounts	Adjusted Basis	F.M.V
Cash	$ 45,000	$ 45,000	J	$190,000	$180,000
Accounts Receivable	0	$ 60,000	K	$190,000	$180,000
Store Building (for sale)	$150,000	$180,000	L	$190,000	$180,000
Office Building (for rent)	$375,000	$240,000			
Goodwill, etc.	0	$ 15,000			
	$570,000	$540,000		$570,000	$540,000

(a) This year the LLC collected the accounts receivable and sold the store building for $210,000. What are the tax consequences to Karen's estate?

(b) Can the LLC make a § 754 election as a result of Karen's death? If so, what are the tax consequences to Karen's estate upon the collection of the accounts receivable and sale of the store building for $210,000? Taking into account all of the facts, would a § 754 election be beneficial?

PART II

TAXATION OF CORPORATIONS AND SHAREHOLDERS

CHAPTER 10

TAXATION OF CORPORATE INCOME AND IDENTIFYING TAXABLE CORPORATE ENTITIES

SECTION 2. IDENTIFYING TAXABLE CORPORATE ENTITIES

A. WHAT IS A "CORPORATION" UNDER THE INCOME TAX

1. Anne and Bill plan to form a limited liability company to engage in the business of developing and marketing computer software. They have identified between 35 and 50 potential investors who will contribute varying amounts of cash for membership interests totaling approximately 75% - 85% of profits and losses (after Anne and Bill receive handsome salaries). Under the governing state law, the LLC

may be member-managed or manager-managed, membership interests may be freely transferable or nontransferable, and the LLC may or may not be dissolved by the death, bankruptcy, retirement, or expulsion of a member, all as provided in the LLC agreement. Anne and Bill want the LLC to be managed by themselves, with the investors having only the minimal rights of members required by state law. Only Anne and Bill will have authority to act on behalf of the LLC. Because of the limited powers that the investor-members will be granted, Anne and Bill think it best that the investors be permitted to sell or assign their membership interests if they so desire, although Anne and Bill think that the actual opportunities for resale will be limited by market forces. Of course, Anne and Bill want the business of the LLC to be uninterrupted by the death, bankruptcy, etc. of an investor-member. Will the LLC be taxed as a corporation if organized in the manner contemplated by Anne and Bill?

2. (a) Rabbit Battery Manufacturing Corp. formed two wholly owned limited liability companies Cadmium Disposal LLC and Mercury Recycling LLC. What is the effect, if any, on Rabbit's taxable income if Cadmium Disposal has net losses of $2,000,000 this year and Mercury Recycling has net income of $3,000,000.

   (b) Rabbit Battery Manufacturing Corp. has a wholly owned subsidiary, Cadmium Disposal, Inc. Rabbit owns 8 of ten membership units in Mercury Recycling LLC, a limited liability company, in which Cadmium Disposal owns the other 2 membership units. What is the effect, if any, on Rabbit's taxable income if Cadmium Disposal has net losses of $2,000,000 this year and Mercury Recycling has net income of $3,000,000?

B. REGARD AND DISREGARD OF THE CORPORATE ENTITY

1. Donald Dudley and Webster Dudley are local real estate developers, well known for developing Spindletop Industrial Park, Calumet Garden Apartments, the Moreford & McAdams Office Tower, and numerous other projects. The Dudleys generally conduct their business as a partnership under the name Dudley Brothers Construction Co. They have found in recent years that when they attempt to obtain options for, or title to, various parcels of real estate in order to put together a suitable tract for development, the owners, knowing the partnership's reputation, usually demand quite a high price for their real estate. The partners therefore propose in the future to organize a corporation for each new development, hoping thereby to disguise the identity of the partnership, and in that way obtain options or title to property at a lower price. Immediately after such a corporation, acting as a nominee for the Dudley brothers, has obtained all options or land necessary for development, the options or the land will be conveyed to the partnership for development.

The corporations will never issue any stock except for qualifying shares. The funds necessary to acquire the options or land will be contributed to the corporation by the partnership as a capital contribution as necessary. There will be only an initial meeting of each of the corporations. At that meeting the Dudleys will be elected directors and officers of the corporation and will then authorize and execute an agreement between the corporation and Dudley Brothers Construction Company providing that the corporation is only a nominee of the partnership, and that immediately upon obtaining all options or land necessary for the development title to such options or land will be conveyed to Dudley Brothers Construction Company.

The Dudley brothers have asked our advice whether the corporations will be taxed as separate corporations or whether they will be ignored for tax purposes and all of their activities attributed to Dudley Brothers Construction Company under the following fact patterns:

(a) A corporation might obtain the land and some period of time may elapse between the acquisition and the commencement of construction. To minimize carrying costs, after the acquisition but prior to transferring title of the land to Dudley Brothers Construction Company upon commencement of construction, the corporation will lease out the vacant land. For example, rural land may be rented out for farming and city land may be rented out to another company to run a parking lot. The nominee corporation would simply receive rents, deposit checks to a bank account, and immediately pay the rent over to Dudley Brothers Construction Company using its own checks.

(b) One or more of the corporations would acquire fee simple title and/or options on the land in its own name, and upon completing the acquisition would immediately transfer title to the land and/or the options to the partnership.

C. REALLOCATION OF INCOME

1. Georgia owns all of the stock of Malific Xenophobe Oil Distributing Corporation, which not only has not shown a profit, but has consistently lost money in every year since Georgia acquired the stock. Georgia also conducted an oil and gas equipment leasing business as a sole proprietor. Georgia's largest drilling rig normally leases for $1,000 a day. Recently Malific Xenophobe used Georgia's drilling rig for 60 days, and because Malific Xenophobe reserves and credit were insufficient to permit it to both pay its workers and pay Georgia $60,000, Georgia rented the drilling rig to Malific Xenophobe for the 60 days for $5,000. What are the tax consequences to Georgia and Malific Xenophobe?

CHAPTER 11

FORMATION OF THE CORPORATION

SECTION 1. RECEIPT OF STOCK FOR PROPERTY

A. BASIC PRINCIPLES

1. Amy and Ben plan to organize X Corporation to engage in the construction business. Amy will contribute a truck with a fair market value of $150,000 and a basis of $50,000 and a power shovel with a basis of $125,000 and a fair market value of $100,000 in exchange for 20 shares of voting common stock. Ben will contribute $100,000 in cash and undeveloped land, previously held as an investment, having a fair market value of $150,000 a basis of $20,000, in exchange for 100 shares of $1,000 par value nonvoting preferred stock with an 8 percent dividend preference and 12 shares of voting common stock. The fair market value of the preferred stock is $100,000. What are the tax consequences to Amy, Ben and X Corporation as a result of the formation of the corporation? Specifically, how much, if any, gain must each recognize; what is the basis to each shareholder in the stock received; and what is the corporation's basis in the assets received by it?

2. (a) Claire and Don formed Y Corporation to engage in the waste hauling and landfill business. Claire contributed a solid waste truck with a basis of $150,000 and a fair market value of $100,000 in exchange for 10 shares of voting common stock. Don contributed land with a basis of $30,000 and a fair market value of $100,000 in exchange for 10 shares of voting common stock. What are the tax consequences to Claire, Don and Y Corporation as a result of the formation of the corporation?

   (b) Suppose alternatively that Claire contributed a solid waste truck with a basis of $150,000 and a fair market value of $100,000 and a liquid waste truck with a basis of $60,000 and a fair market value of $100,000 in exchange for 20 shares of voting common stock. Don contributed land with a basis of $30,000 and a fair market value of $200,000 in exchange for 20 shares of voting common stock. What are the tax consequences to Claire, Don and Y Corporation as a result of the formation of the corporation?

(c) Suppose alternatively that Claire contributed a solid waste truck with a basis of $150,000 and a fair market value of $100,000, a liquid waste truck with a basis of $40,000 and a fair market value of $100,000, and a bulldozer with a basis of $75,000 and a fair market value of $50,000, in exchange for 25 shares of voting common stock. Don contributed land with a basis of $30,000 and a fair market value of $250,000 in exchange for 25 shares of voting common stock. What are the tax consequences to Claire, Don and Y Corporation as a result of the formation of the corporation?

3. Ed, Fran, and Georgie formed Z Corporation. Ed transferred 1,000 shares of stock of Specific Motors, Inc. with a basis of $150,000 and a fair market value of $100,000. Fran transferred 500 shares of stock of Worldwide Business Machines, Inc. with a fair market value of $100,000 and a basis of $20,000. Georgie transferred 2,000 shares of stock of Pear Computer Corporation with a fair market value of $100,000 and a basis of $5,000. Ed, Fran, and Georgie each received 10 shares of Z Corporation stock. Specific Motors, Worldwide Business Machines, and Pear Computer Corporation are all traded on the New York Stock Exchange. What are the tax consequences to Ed, Fran, Georgie, and Z Corporation as a result of the formation of the corporation?

B. "PROPERTY" AND MIDSTREAM TRANSFERS OF INCOME

1. Alicia and Bart are the sole shareholders of X Corporation, which is engaged in a financial services business. Alicia and Bart each own 50 shares of common stock. Alicia contributed a § 453 installment note with a basis of $20,000 and a fair market value of $100,000 to X Corporation in exchange for 10 shares of stock worth $100,000. Alicia received the note earlier this year in exchange for land that she had held for investment for many years. Bart, who has a real estate license but does not actively conduct any real estate brokerage business, contributed a cash method account receivable in the amount of $15,000, which arose from brokering a commercial lease on behalf of a friend who owned an office building. Bart also contributed a parcel of land held for sale to customers in the ordinary course of his unincorporated real estate development business, which had a fair market value of $85,000 and a basis of $20,000, and which was subject to a binding executory purchase and sale contract. In exchange, Bart received in exchange 10 shares of stock worth $100,000. What are the tax consequences to Alicia, Bart and X Corporation as a result of the formation of the corporation?

C. "SOLELY FOR STOCK" – THE RECEIPT OF OTHER PROPERTY

1. Claire, Don, and Erin plan to organize a corporation to engage in the construction business. They will each make the following contributions in exchange for the specified interest in the corporation. What are the tax consequences to each of the investors and to the corporation as a result of the formation of the corporation? Specifically, how much, if any, gain must each recognize; what is the character of the gain; what is the basis to shareholder in the stock or promissory note received; and what is the corporation's basis in the assets received by it?

   (a) Claire will contribute construction supplies previously held for sale to customers in the ordinary course of business, with a fair market value of $450,000 and a basis of $300,000, in exchange for 20 shares of common stock and a promissory note for $200,000 due in 10 years, with interest at the prime rate payable semi-annually.

   (b) Don will contribute a bulldozer with a fair market value of $180,000 and an adjusted basis of $300,000 and a cement mixer truck with an adjusted basis of $150,000 and a fair market value of $270,000 in exchange for 20 shares of common stock and a promissory note for $200,000 due in 10 years, with interest at the prime rate payable semi-annually. All of the gain inherent in the cement mixer is subject to § 1245 recapture.

   (c) Erin will contribute land and a building previously held out for rental. The land has a basis of $60,000 and the building an adjusted basis of $210,000. Their combined fair market value is $450,000. The building is not subject to either § 1245 or § 1250 recapture. Erin will receive 20 shares of common stock and a promissory note for $200,000 due in ten years, with interest at the prime rate payable semi-annually.

      (1) Assume that the land has a fair market value of $90,000 and the building a fair market value of $360,000.

      (2) Assume alternatively that the land has a fair market value of $180,000 and the building a fair market value of $270,000.

2. Fran, Glenn, and Helen formed Y Corporation by making the following transfers. Fran and Glenn each transferred $100,000 of cash and received 100 shares each of common stock. Helen transferred unimproved real estate with a basis of $25,000 and received 20 shares of common stock, worth $20,000, and Y Corporation's note for $80,000 payable in twenty-one years, with interest payable annually at 6 % (which you should assume is adequate stated interest).

   (a) What are the tax consequences to Helen? What is Helen's basis in the Y Corporation stock? What is Y Corporation's basis in the land?

(b) How would your answer change if Helen received 10 shares of common stock, having an aggregate fair market value of $20,000, and 80 shares of $1,000 par preferred stock, which paid a dividend of 6 % annually and is redeemable in 21 years at the option of either Y Corporation or Helen? The preferred stock had an aggregate fair market value of $80,000.

(c) Would your answer change if the 80 shares of $1,000 par preferred stock Helen received was sinking fund preferred stock redeemable in twenty years at the option of either Y Corporation or Helen?

SECTION 2. "SOLELY" FOR STOCK: ASSUMPTION OF LIABILITIES

A. BASIC PRINCIPLES

1. Frank and Jessie plan to organize a corporation to operate a college textbook store, which will be named Fleecem Folios, Ltd. They will each engage in the exchanges described below. What are the tax consequences to Frank and Jessie, and Fleecem Folios that result from the formation of the corporation? Specifically, how much, if any, gain must each recognize; what is the basis to each shareholder in the stock received; and what is the corporation's basis in the assets received by it?

(a) Frank will contribute 10,000 law school text books, previously held for sale to customers in the ordinary course of business, with a fair market value of $450,000 and a basis of $300,000, in exchange for 10 shares of common stock, worth $250,000. In addition, the corporation will assume $200,000 of Frank debts that are secured by a perfected purchase money security interest in the books.

(b) Jessie will contribute land previously held as an investment on which the new corporation will build a store. The land has a fair market value of $350,000 and a basis of $260,000. Jessie will receive 10 shares of common stock and the corporation will assume a $100,000 debt Jessie owed to the First National Bank of Northfield.

(1)(i) Assume that Jessie's debt was incurred four years ago to pay gambling debts incurred in Atlantic City and is unsecured.

(ii) Assume alternatively that Jessie's debt to the First National Bank of Northfield was secured by a mortgage on the land.

(2) Assume alternatively that the land was used as a parking lot and Jessie's debt was unsecured but was incurred last year to fund

deductible operating expenses of the now failed sole proprietorship parking lot business in connection with which Jessie previously had used the land.

2. Al, Bev, and Carl each owned one third of the outstanding stock of X Corporation. Al, Bev, and Carl owned Blackacre as equal tenants in common. Blackacre had a fair market value of $450,000 and was subject to a nonrecourse purchase money mortgage of $450,000. Each of Al, Bev, and Carl had a basis in the respective undivided one-third interests of $170,000. Al, Bev and Carl contributed Blackacre to X Corporation. What are the tax consequences?

B. LIABILITIES IN EXCESS OF BASIS

(1) GENERAL RULES

1. (a) Bonnie and Clyde formed FastGetaway Corporation to engage in a limousine charter service business. Bonnie contributed $50,000 in cash. Clyde contributed a Mercedes-Benz limousine with a fair market value of $80,000 and a basis of $10,000, subject to a purchase money lien indebtedness of $30,000, which was assumed by the corporation. What are the tax consequences to Clyde and the corporation?

   (b) Assume alternatively that Bonnie contributed $100,000 in cash. Clyde contributed a Mercedes-Benz limousine with a fair market value of $80,000 and a basis of $12,000, subject to a purchase money lien indebtedness of $25,000, which was assumed by the corporation, and a Lincoln limousine with a fair market value of $60,000 and a basis of $48,000, subject to a purchase money lien indebtedness of $15,000, which was assumed by the corporation. What are the tax consequences to Clyde and the corporation?

2. Oscar and Patty formed NHC Corporation. Oscar contributed $250,000 in cash in exchange for 10 shares of common stock. Patty contributed land and a warehouse building. The land has a basis of $10,000 and the building has an adjusted basis of $30,000. The fair market value of the land is $87,500. The fair market value of the building is $262,500. Patty received 10 shares of common stock and the corporation assumed a $100,000 purchase money mortgage secured by the land and building. What are the tax consequences to Patty and the corporation?

3. (a) Evan and William formed Barleycorn Corporation to engage in the distilling business. Evan contributed $250,000 in cash and William contributed land and a warehouse building previously held out for rental. The land had a basis of $10,000 and the building had an adjusted basis of $30,000. The fair market value of land is $87,500, and the fair market value of the building is $262,500. William will

receive 10 shares of common and stock and the corporation will take the property subject to $100,000 nonrecourse purchase money mortgage lien, but it will not expressly assume the mortgage indebtedness. What are the tax consequences to William and the corporation?

(b) Would answer differ if the mortgage was a recourse mortgage and the corporation did not expressly assume the mortgage?

(c) How would your answer in part (a) differ if the fair market value of land was $10,000, and the fair market value of the building was $340,000?

4. Edmund and Tenzig formed Sasquatch Corporation. Tenzig contributed $3,000,000 of cash in exchange for 75 shares of common stock. Edmund contributed land with a fair market value of $2,000,000 and a basis of $800,000, subject to a $1,500,000 nonrecourse mortgage debt, and Edmund's negotiable promissory note payable to the order of Sasquatch Corporation, in the amount of $500,000, in exchange for 25 shares of common stock. Edmund's note bore interest at the prime rate plus 2 percent, payable annually, with $100,000 of principal due on each of the first five anniversaries of the date of the note. What are the tax consequences to Edmund and to Sasquatch Corporation?

(2) ASSUMPTION OF DEBTS THAT WOULD BE DEDUCTIBLE WHEN PAID: SECTION 357(c)(3)

1. Jack and Abe, who have been conducting separate lobbying businesses in Washington, D.C. as sole proprietors for several years have joined together and to incorporate their business as Payoff Peddlers Corp. Each of them received 10 shares of common stock.

   Jack, who has operated his business on the cash method, contributed the following assets:

Asset	Basis	F.M.V.
Accounts Receivable	$ 0	$ 60,000
Office Equipment	$28,000	$ 40,000
Total	$28,000	$100,000

   In addition, Payoff Peddlers assumed $55,000 of accounts payable (§ 162 expenses) of Jack's sole proprietorship and a $25,000 purchase money loan on the office equipment.

   Abe, who has operated his business on the accrual method, contributed the following assets:

Asset	Basis	F.M.V.
Accounts Receivable	$60,000	$ 60,000
Office Equipment	$28,000	$ 40,000
Total	$88,000	$100,000

In addition, Payoff Peddlers assumed $55,000 of accounts payable (§ 162 expenses) of Abe's sole proprietorship and a $25,000 purchase money loan on the office equipment.

As permitted by § 448(b)(2), Payoff Peddlers elected to use the cash method. Following incorporation, it collected all of the accounts receivable and paid all of the accounts payable.

(a) What are the tax consequences to Jack, Abe, and Payoff Peddlers upon incorporation?

(b) Who is taxable upon collection of the accounts receivable?

(c) To what extent may Payoff Peddlers deduct payment of the accounts payable?

2. Jeff and Louis started Border-on-the-Nile.com, Inc. to market and sell books over the internet. Each received 10 shares of common stock. Jeff contributed $200,000 in cash. Louis, who is an accrual method taxpayer, contributed an inventory of books worth $250,000, with a basis of $40,000. In addition, the corporation agreed to pay a $50,000 prize to whoever holds the winning lottery ticket from a contest run by Louis in his former bricks-and-mortar-based bookstore business. All of the tickets have been distributed, but the winner has not yet been drawn. Pursuant to § 461(h), and the regulations thereunder, Louis's deduction for the $50,000 prize is not allowed until economic performance, which in this case is payment of the prize money to the winner. What are the tax consequences to Louis and Border-on-the-Nile.com?

3. Toxic Chemical Corp. formed a new wholly owned subsidiary, Chimera, Inc. by transferring Brownacre, land that is the site of an arsenic mine formerly operated by Toxic, with a gross fair market value of $500,000 and with a basis of $300,000 in exchange for common stock. Chimera agreed to be responsible for any and all future environmental remediation expenses with respect to the property that might be required by the Federal EPA or the state Department of Environmental Protection. Toxic estimated that the future environmental remediation expenses would be approximately $400,000. Shortly thereafter, Toxic sold the Chimera stock for $100,000. What are the tax consequences to Toxic?

SECTION 3. THE CONTROL REQUIREMENT

1. Bill owned a copyright on a computer software program, with a fair market value of $10,000,000 and a basis of $1,000. Bill transferred the copyright on the program to newly formed Doors Corporation in exchange for all 30,000 shares of voting common stock. Doors was unable to further develop and market the software without the investment of significant additional capital. To this end, pursuant to a prearranged plan, three months later Merrill-Goldman, an investment banking house, sold $40,000,000 par value nonvoting preferred stock of Doors Corporation to public investors on behalf of Doors. As agreed upon in the contract between Doors and Merrill-Goldman, upon completion of the public offering, Doors issued 10,000 shares of common stock to Merrill-Goldman. What are the tax consequences to Bill and to Doors?

2. (a) Donald Thump owned a hotel property consisting of land and a building. The fair market value of the land was $1,000,000 and the basis of the land was $100,000; the fair market value of the building was $19,000,000, its adjusted basis was $8,000,0000 and it original cost (unadjusted basis before depreciation) was $22,000,000. In January, the Tripletree Hotel Corporation, offered to purchase Donald's hotel for $20,000,000. The offer was open until April 15. On February 15th, pursuant to advice from his C.P.A., Ernie Whinney, Donald transferred the land and building to newly formed Apprentice Corp. in exchange for all 100 shares of its stock. On March 1st, Donald counter-offered to Tripletree's offer, stating that he would accept $19,500,000 in exchange for all of the stock of Apprentice Corp. This offer was accepted by Tripletree and the deal was closed on April 1st. Ernie Whinney has advised Donald that the incorporation of Tripletree was tax-free under § 351. Is he correct?

   (b) Suppose alternatively, that after transferring the hotel to Apprentice Corp. in exchange for all of its stock, pursuant to a pre-arranged plan, Donald transferred all of the stock of Apprentice to Las Margaritas, Inc., in exchange for 100 shares of stock. Simultaneously, Jose Cuervo, who theretofore had owned all 200 shares of the stock of Las Margaritas, transferred to Las Margaritas a restaurant building with a fair market value of $4,000,000 and a basis of $500,000, in exchange for 20 additional shares of stock. What are the tax consequences to Donald?

3. Paducah Oil Company has recently acquired a chain of gas stations previously operated by Leviathan Oil Corp. in Kentucky, following Leviathan's decision to cease its marketing operations there. In addition to the seventy-five company owned gas stations acquired from Leviathan by Paducah, Leviathan had an additional one hundred or so

independent retailers that owned their own gas stations and purchased gasoline from Leviathan Oil.

Paducah plans to convert all of the seventy-five gas stations that it acquired from Leviathan to convenience grocery store-gas stations that it will operate under the trade name BlueCat, but which will sell gasoline refined by Paducah. The management of Paducah believes that outlet name recognition would be enhanced, and hence average profits per store would be enhanced, if substantially more than seventy-five BlueCat stores were operated in Kentucky. Additionally, it is looking for additional outlets for its refined products.

To accomplish these goals the management of Paducah plans to form a subsidiary, BlueCat Stores, Inc., to which it will contribute all of the seventy-five gas stations that it purchased from Leviathan, some cash, and a quantity of refined petroleum products. In exchange, Paducah will receive one hundred percent of the voting common stock of BlueCat. Immediately thereafter, Paducah will offer to exchange with the one hundred independent dealers previously selling Leviathan gasoline in Kentucky a number of its shares of BlueCat equal to the fair market value of each of their respective businesses, in consideration of the transfer directly to BlueCat of all of their business assets, including their gasoline stations, inventory, customer accounts, etc. It is anticipated that if all of the independent owners accept the offer, in the aggregate the previously independent owners will hold a fifty percent interest in BlueCat. No individual owner, however, will hold more than two or three percent of the BlueCat stock. The owners will continue to operate their stations as managers of the convenience stores and will receive salaries, bonuses and fringe benefits from BlueCat.

The management of Paducah is concerned whether this transaction will be a tax-free incorporation. Although Paducah's cost basis for the seventy-five gas stations is not substantially less than fair market value, BlueCat will be a going concern and its stock, therefore, may have a value in excess of the fair market value of the underlying assets. Additionally, the refined gasoline to be contributed has a value substantially in excess of its basis. More importantly, however, Paducah wants to be able to assure the independent retailers that they will not owe any income taxes as a result of the exchange of their business assets for BlueCat stock. If the exchanges are taxable, Paducah is concerned that the station owners may prefer to sell for cash or debt instruments and the Paducah management would prefer not to use a cash or debt acquisition route.

Will § 351 will apply to the incorporation of BlueCat Stores, Inc?

SECTION 4. RECEIPT OF STOCK FOR SERVICES

1. (a) Alberto, Beryl, and Chris have been operating a fashion design business (as a partnership) under the name Ritzy Rags for the past several years. Because they are planning to expand to manufacturing, Alberto, Beryl, and Chris are planning to incorporate the business. Debby, an employee who is one of the nation's hottest fashion designers, has been an important factor in the success of the business. Recently Debby received an offer from another apparel company that included stock and stock options in a compensation package. To induce Debby to remain with Ritzy Rags, Alberto, Beryl, and Chris have offered her twenty-five percent of the common stock of the new Ritzy Rags Corporation, to which the business will be transferred. Advise the parties regarding the tax consequences of the incorporation transaction.

   (b) What if Debby's stock must be sold back to Ritzy Rags for $10 per share if her employment terminates any time in the next four years?

   (c) What if Debby doesn't receive any stock in Ritzy Rags immediately upon its incorporation, but receives an option to purchase from the corporation at any time in the next five years an amount of stock equal to the number of shares originally received by each of Alberto, Beryl and Chris (i.e., if Alberto, Beryl and Chris each received 100 shares, Debby would have an option for 100 shares) at the same price paid by Alberto, Beryl and Chris?

2. (a) Fran, Les, Pat, and Sean plan to organize a corporation to engage in the construction business. Fran will contribute $400,000 in cash for 40 shares of common stock. Les will contribute equipment with a fair market value of $200,000 and a basis of $90,000 for 20 shares of common stock. Pat will contribute building materials with a fair market value of $200,000 and a basis of $210,000 for 20 shares of common stock. Sean will contribute a contract with Falls City University for the construction by Sean or Sean's assignee of a new Dental School building, a letter of intent from the University of the Bluegrass to enter into a contract with Sean or Sean's assignee for construction of a new Engineering School building, and Sean's services in organizing the corporation and supervising the construction of the two buildings. Sean will receive 20 shares of common stock.

   What are the tax consequences to each of the shareholders and to the corporation of the formation of the corporation?

   (b) How might your answer to (a) differ if Fran were to receive participating preferred stock instead of common stock? Does it matter whether the participating preferred stock has voting rights to elect directors?

3. Ellen, Fred, Ginny, and Hank plan to form X Corporation. Ellen, Fred, and Ginny are contributing appreciated property. Hank is contributing only services. Under which of the following alternative capital structures will the incorporation qualify under § 351.

(a) (1) Ellen, Fred, and Ginny collectively receive 80 shares of Class A $1,000 par value, 7%, voting participating preferred stock and Hank receives 20 shares of Class B voting common stock. The Class A participating preferred stock is entitled to a cumulative 7% preferred dividend and a $1,000 per share liquidation preference. After the Class A preference has been satisfied, both Class A and Class B stock share equally, share-by-share, in all current and liquidating distributions.

(2) What if Hank's Class B common stock was nonvoting?

(3) Ellen, Fred, and Ginny's Class A stock was voting common stock and Hank's 20 shares of Class B stock was $1,000 par value, 7%, nonvoting limited and preferred stock.

(4) Ellen, Fred, and Ginny collectively received 80 shares of voting common stock and Hank received a $20,000 bond (promissory note), convertible at any time in the next four years into 40 shares of voting common stock.

(b) Ellen, Fred, and Ginny collectively receive 80 shares of Class A voting common stock and 80 shares of Class B nonvoting common stock. Hank receives 20 shares of Class A voting common stock and 20 shares of Class C nonvoting preferred stock.

(c) Ellen, Fred, and Ginny collectively receive 75 shares of Class A voting common stock and Hank receives 25 shares of Class B voting common stock. The only difference between the shares is that the Class A stock elects four directors and the Class B stock elects one director.

CHAPTER 12

THE CAPITAL STRUCTURE OF THE CORPORATION

SECTION 1. DEBT VERSUS EQUITY

1. Howard Cunningham and John Walton have decided to combine their respective sole proprietorships, Cunningham's Hardware Store and Walton's Lumber Mill, into a corporation to be named Milwaukee Mountain Lumber & Hardware Supply, Inc. (MML&HS). Each will contribute the land, buildings, inventory, and accounts receivable of their respective businesses. MML&HS will assume all outstanding mortgages and accounts payable of both businesses, which total $2,500,000. The net assets of each business are worth $400,000. Additional capital to expand the business will be provided by Joan B. Tipton, who will contribute $400,000 cash. Cunningham, Walton and Tipton each will receive 100 shares of MML&HS common stock. The corporation will immediately borrow $2,000,000 from the Usury Bank & Trust Co. and will refinance the preexisting $2,500,000 debt into a $4,500,000 note. The note will bear interest at prime rate plus two percent, adjusted quarterly, with the principal due in ten years, and the note will be secured by a mortgage on the property of the corporation.

   After the contribution and the new borrowing, the gross assets of the corporation will be $5,700,000; the net assets of the corporation will be $1,200,000; and the corporation's basis in its assets (other than cash) will be $2,500,000.

   MML&HS will require an additional $4,500,000 to expand its operations. Barbara Beancounter, CPA, who has been advising Cunningham, Walton, and Tipton regarding the formation of MML&HS up to now has presented a number of alternative proposals for raising the additional $4,500,000. She has advised the incorporators that any of these plans will secure an interest deduction for the corporation, as well as avoiding dividend treatment to Cunningham, Walton, and Tipton with respect to any distributions that they receive. Evaluate each of the following alternative proposals to determine if the instruments will be accorded debt treatment by the IRS and the Courts.

(a) Cunningham, Walton and Tipton will each loan MML&HS $1,500,000 and receive a five-year note, with interest at one percent below prime, adjusted and payable annually.

(b) Cunningham, Walton and Tipton will each loan MML&HS $1,500,000 and receive a twenty-year subordinated income note with interest at ten percent payable annually only out of net profits of the corporation.

(c) Usury Bank & Trust will loan MML&HS an additional $4,500,000, but will require the personal guarantee of the shareholders who will be jointly and severally liable. Does it matter whether the loan is adequately secured by corporate assets? What if the loan is unsecured with respect to the corporation, but secured by personal assets of the shareholders?

(d) Tipton will loan the corporation $4,500,000 and receive a five-year note, with interest at one percent below prime, adjusted and payable annually. What will happen if two years later MML&HS experiences cash flow problems and stops paying interest on the note?

(e) The spouse of each shareholder will loan the corporation $1,500,000 and receive a five-year note, with interest at one percent below prime, adjusted and payable annually.

2. Macrosoft Corp. is a small computer software development business established a few years ago by Bernie and Mike, who contributed a total of $400,000 cash to capitalize Macrosoft. As a result of subsequent stock issues to Bernie (for an additional $200,000) and to employees of the corporation (in lieu of cash bonuses when the corporation was nearly bankrupt a few years ago), Bernie now owns 45 percent of the stock, Mike owns 20 percent, and 35 percent is owned by sixty different employees, none of whom holds more than 1% of the stock. The aggregate value of the stock of Macrosoft, which is not publicly traded, is about $5,000,000, but if Macrosoft does not keep pace with the development of new software, it could be bankrupt within a year. The corporation requires approximately $1,000,000 to fund new research and has devised the following plan:

   (a) Bernie will lend the corporation $200,000. The loan will be represented by a promissory note due in ten years, and will bear interest at the prime rate, plus three percent, compounded and due semi-annually.

   (b) Mike will lend the corporation $100,000 for one year, at the prime rate, and purchase 100 shares of $300 dollar par value preferred stock for $300,000.

(c) Ivan Milkem, a venture capitalist, will purchase $400,000 worth of common stock.

SECTION 2. BOND DISCOUNT AND PREMIUM

1. X Corp. is planning to issue bonds to raise cash to expand its business operations. Consider the following transactions.

   (a) On June 30th of the current year X Corp. issues $100,000 face value bonds due in 10 years, which pay zero stated interest, for an issue price of $37,688.95. How much interest may X Corp. deduct during the current year and the next year?

   (b) On June 30th, X Corp. issues for cash $100,000, ten-year bonds that bear interest at the prime rate plus 1%, which you may assume for all relevant periods computes to 6%. Interest is payable semiannually. The applicable federal rate for the current year is 7%. How much interest may X Corp. deduct in the current year?

   (c) On June 30th, X Corp. issues $100,000 ten-year bonds bearing interest at 10%, payable semi-annually, but no interest is due and payable until the second anniversary of the bond issue. The applicable federal rate is 7%. How do you determine whether the bonds are OID instruments?

   (d) X Corp. issues $100,000 ten-year convertible bonds. Each bond is convertible into X Corp. common stock at any time prior to redemption at an exchange ratio of one share of stock for $10. When the bonds were issued, X Corp. stock was trading on the stock exchange at 9-7/8 per share. The bonds pay interest annually at 7%. The applicable federal rate was 7% when the bonds were issued. Are the bonds OID bonds?

2. Empire Realty Development Corp. purchased the Palace Hotel from Don. In exchange for the Palace, Don received an Empire bond in the face amount of $5,000,000 due in ten years. No express interest is due on the bond. At the time of the sale the applicable federal rate was 7%.

   (a) What is Empire's basis for the Palace? If the deal closed on June 30th, how much interest may Empire deduct in the year of the sale?

   (b) Suppose that the stated principal amount of the bond was $5,000,000 and interest accrued at 7% compounded semi-annually, but no interest was payable until the bond was due in 10 years. At that time, Don was to receive the $5,000,000 principal and $4,948,944 of interest, for a total amount due of $9,948,944. How much interest must

Don include and how much interest may Empire deduct for the year of sale?

(c) Suppose that the stated principal amount of the bond was $2,342,112 and interest accrued at 15% compounded semi-annually, but no interest was payable until the bond was due in 10 years. At that time, Don was to receive the $2,342,112 principal and $7,606,831 of interest, for a total amount due of $9,948,944. How much interest must Don include and how much interest may Empire deduct for the year of sale? Do you need to know whether Empire uses the cash method or the accrual method in order to answer the question?

3. On July 1, 2014, Adam Smith purchased a newly issued $100,000 debt instrument issued by the Pari-Mutuel Insurance Company, Inc. The stated terms of the bond provided for annual interest at 10%, payable semiannually with the principal due on June 30, 2024. Because interest rates had fallen between the time the bonds and the prospectus were printed, to adjust for the higher than market stated interest rate, the bonds were sold for $102,500. What are the tax consequences to Adam when he receives $5,000 of interest in 2014? When he receives $10,000 of interest in 2015? When he receives the $100,000 principal payment in 2024?

CHAPTER 13

DIVIDEND DISTRIBUTIONS

SECTION 2. DIVIDEND DISTRIBUTIONS IN GENERAL

1. Bugs-Я-Us Corporation is an accrual method taxpayer engaged in a local pest control business. Last year it had the following receipts and expenses. Compute its earnings and profits. Assume that the corporate tax rate is a flat rate of 20%.

   Receipts

Gross receipts from exterminating services	$106,000
Dividend income	$ 10,000
Interest on municipal bonds	$ 5,000
Capital gain	$ 4,000
Additional capital contribution by shareholders	$ 2,000
	$127,000

   Expenses

Wages, rent & supplies	$ 33,000
Fines payable for violation of state law	$ 4,000
Depreciation on equipment (would have been only $3,000 under § 168(g))	$ 6,000
Section 179 deduction for machinery purchase	$ 10,000
Interest on loan to buy municipal bonds	$ 3,000
Capital losses	$ 5,000
	$ 61,000

   What are Bugs-Я-Us Corporation's earnings and profits for the taxable year?

2. Determine the amount of the dividend received by the shareholders of Benny's Bait Shop & Sushi Bar, Inc. in each of the following situations and the consequences of any distributions that are not dividends.

   (a) Ben owns all of the stock of Benny's Bait Shop & Sushi Bar, Inc. His basis in the stock is $24,000. In its first year of existence, Benny's Bait Shop & Sushi Bar, Inc. earned $30,000 of earnings and profits. One-half of this sum was earned in the period January to June; the other half was earned in July through December. On July 1, Benny's

Bait Shop & Sushi Bar borrowed $50,000 from the Usury National Bank and distributed $40,000 to Ben.

(b) Assume that in its first year of business Benny's Bait Shop & Sushi Bar lost $20,000, measured by earnings and profits. In its second year of existence, Benny's Bait Shop & Sushi Bar earned $24,000 of earnings and profits and distributed $15,000 to Ben.

(c) Assume that after several years of operation Benny's Bait Shop & Sushi Bar had $36,000 of accumulated earnings and profits. During the current year, Benny's Bait Shop & Sushi Bar earned an additional $24,000 of earnings and profits. On April 1, Benny's Bait Shop & Sushi Bar distributed $40,000 to Ben. On July 1, Ben sold half of his Benny's Bait Shop & Sushi Bar stock to Molly for $50,000. On December 31, Benny's Bait Shop & Sushi Bar distributed $20,000 to each of Ben and Molly.

(d)(1) Assume (as in problem (c)) that after several years of operation Benny's Bait Shop & Sushi Bar had $36,000 of accumulated earnings and profits. During the current year Benny's Bait Shop & Sushi Bar has a $32,000 loss (as measured by current earnings and profits) from ordinary business operations. On April 1, Benny's Bait Shop & Sushi Bar distributed $40,000 to Ben. On July 1, Ben sold half of his Benny's Bait Shop & Sushi Bar stock to Molly for $50,000. On December 31, Benny's Bait Shop & Sushi Bar distributed $20,000 to each of Ben and Molly. What are the consequences to Ben and Molly. What are the corporation's accumulated earnings and profits at the beginning of the next year?

(2) Assume alternatively that Benny's Bait Shop & Sushi Bar's $32,000 loss this year was entirely attributable to the sale of a single § 1231 asset on February 1 and that ordinary business operations for the year were exactly break-even. Does your answer change?

3. Glowing Waters Nuclear Electric Power Corp. has 100,000 shares of $1,000 par value, 7% dividend, preferred stock and 100,000 shares of common stock outstanding. Glowing Waters has no accumulated earnings and profits and this year had current earnings and profits of $850,000. It distributed $700,000 on the preferred stock and $250,000 on the common stock. How much of each distribution should be treated as a dividend?

4. Alice owns 900 shares of common stock of E-Machines Computer Corp. She purchased 300 shares six years ago for $9,000 and the other 600 shares fifteen years ago for $2,000. The corporation, which is publicly traded, made a distribution, which was a dividend under state law, of $11 on each share. Alice received $9,900. Because E-Machines

Computer Corp. made aggregate distributions to its shareholders in excess of its combined current and accumulated earnings and profits, it properly sent Alice a Form 1099 stating that the amount of the dividends received was only $3,300. How should Alice treat the other $6,600 that she received?

5. Standard Oil of Alaska, Inc. has a wholly owned subsidiary, Fish Oil Corp. During the current year Standard Oil had accumulated and current earnings and profits totaling $100,000 and Fish Oil had accumulated and current earnings and profits totaling $300,000. Standard Oil distributed $250,000 to its shareholders this year. What portion of the $250,000 distribution constitutes a dividend?

SECTION 3. DISTRIBUTION OF A DIVIDEND IN KIND

What are the tax consequences to each of the distributing corporation and its shareholders in each of the following situations? Assume that all individual taxpayers report on the cash method.

1. (a) Mudville Corp. has $25,000 of accumulated earnings and profits, but no current earnings and profits through December 31st of the current year. On December 31st Mudville Corp. distributes to Casey, its sole shareholder, a parcel of land with a basis of $60,000, which the corporate minutes state was distributed with the intention of distributing property worth $60,000.

   (b) The IRS has audited Mudville Corp.'s income tax return for the year. The only item that the IRS proposes to change is to treat the value of the land as $150,000 instead of $60,000. How will Mudville Corp. and Casey be affected if the IRS prevails on this change?

2. (a) Grand Teton Real Estate Development Corp. has no accumulated or current earnings and profits through December 31st of the current year. On December 31st Grand Teton distributes to Ricardo, its sole shareholder, a parcel of land with a basis of $90,000 and a fair market value of $190,000, subject to a mortgage of $140,000, which Ricardo assumed.

   (b) (1) What if the mortgage was a nonrecourse mortgage and Ricardo took the property subject to the mortgage but did not expressly assume the mortgage?

   (2) What if the nonrecourse mortgage was $200,000?

(c) What if the $140,000 mortgage was a recourse mortgage and Ricardo took the property subject to the mortgage but did not expressly assume the mortgage?

3. (a) At a time when Bassamatic Corp. had accumulated earnings and profits of $140,000 and during a year in which it had no current earnings and profits from operations, Bassamatic Corp. distributed to Yuan, its sole shareholder, land having a fair market value of $100,000 and a basis of $130,000.

   (1) How much loss may Bassamatic Corp. recognize?

   (2) What is the amount of the dividend to Yuan? What is Yuan's basis in the land? How much gain must Yuan recognize if Yuan later sells the land for $180,000?

   (b) What would be the consequences if in (a) Bassamatic sold the land to Yuan for $100,000 and Yuan later sold the land for $180,000? See § 267. What policy reason might there be for the answer being different than in (a)?

4. (a) Omaha Wizard Corp. distributed to Warren, its sole shareholder, 200 shares of stock of Exxon-Mobil Corp., which it purchased on the New York Stock Exchange to hold as an investment. The fair market value of the stock was $100 per share. One hundred of the shares were purchased at $75 per share; the other 100 shares were purchased at $125 per share. Assume that Omaha Wizard Corp.'s accumulated earnings and profits exceed $1,000,000. What are the tax results to Omaha Wizard Corp. and to Warren?

   (b) Insider Corp. distributed to Martha, its sole shareholder, a parcel of real estate consisting of two acres of land and a potpourri factory building. The basis of the land was $400,000 and its fair market value was $2,000,000. The adjusted basis of the building was $3,000,000 and its fair market value was $1,400,000. The property has been held for many years for use in the corporation's business. Insider Corp.'s accumulated earnings and profits are $10,000,000 and it has no current earnings and profits from operations. What are the tax results to Insider Corp. and to Martha?

5. Ophelia owns 25 shares and Hamlet owns 50 shares of common stock of Elsinore Corp., which has 75 shares outstanding. Elsinore Corp. has $115,000 of accumulated earnings and profits and no current earnings and profits from operations. On April 15th, Elsinore Corp. distributed $70,000 of cash to Ophelia. On September 15th Elsinore Corp. distributed to Hamlet land with a basis of $50,000 and a fair market value of $140,000. What is the amount of the dividend received by each

of Hamlet and Ophelia? Assume Elsinore Corp. reports on the cash method.

6. (a) Graceland Corp. has $100,000 of accumulated earnings and profits. The corporation distributes to Elvis, its sole shareholder, a promissory note having a face value of $50,000, due in twenty years, with no stated interest. Assume that $20,000 is the "issue price" of the note under § 1273(b). In general, what are the consequences of the issuance and payment of the note? (Do not bother to make any year-by-year OID computations.)

   (b) What statutory provisions apply to determine the “issue price” of a promissory note issued by a corporation as a dividend? What is the method for determining the “issue price”?

SECTION 4. DISGUISED DIVIDENDS

Do any of the following situations give rise to disguised dividends? If so, how do you determine the amount of the dividend?

1. (a) Wolf and Stein are the shareholders of Mortal Doom Video Games Corp. Wolf owns 60% of the stock and Stein owns 40% of the stock. Mortal Doom is engaged in the design, manufacture, and sale of computer video game software. The corporation has over $20,000,000 of net assets and has 30 employees in addition to Wolf and Stein. Wolf is the vice-president and his salary is $1,200,000 per year. Stein is the president and his salary is $800,000 per year. The corporation had $3,000,000 of profits after payment of Wolf and Stein's salaries.

   (b) Wolf, the 60 percent shareholder, is the president and his salary is $1,200,000 per year. Stein, the 40 percent shareholder, is the vice-president and his salary is $800,000 per year. The corporation had $3,000,000 of profits after payment of Wolf's and Stein's salaries.

   (c) (1) Wolf, the 60 percent shareholder, is the president and his salary is $1,000,000 per year. Stein, the 40 percent shareholder, is the vice-president and his salary is $800,000 per year. The corporation had $30,000 of profits after payment of Wolf and Stein's salaries.

   (2) This year Wolf received a bonus of $1,000,000 and Stein received a bonus of $800,000. The corporation had $4,000,000 of undistributed profits after payment of Wolf's and Stein's salaries and bonuses.

   (3) This year Wolf received a bonus of $1,800,000 and Stein received a bonus of $1,200,000. The corporation had $1,000,000 of

undistributed profits after payment of Wolf and Stein's salaries and bonuses.

(4) This year Wolf received a bonus of $1,200,000 and Stein received a bonus of $600,000. The corporation had $1,200,000 of undistributed profits after payment of Wolf's and Stein's salaries and bonuses.

(d) Would your answers be affected if Mortal Doom Video Games Corp. stock is widely held and traded on the New York Stock Exchange?

2. Ponzi & Company, Inc., an investment banking firm in New York, owns a working horse farm in Lexington, Kentucky. Carla Ponzi, who owns 80% of the stock, and her family have the exclusive use of a mansion located on the horse farm when they visit Lexington during racing season, which is all of April and October. Last year the corporation deducted $48,000 depreciation on the mansion, paid real estate taxes of $12,000 (attributable to the mansion apart from the working farm), and paid utilities and repair bills for the mansion of $24,000. Carla works full-time in the corporation's investment banking business, but performs no services with respect to the horse farm business of the corporation, which is left entirely to a professional manager.

3. Augie owned 100% of the stock of Dog's Breath Saloon & Brew Pub Corp., which has more than $200,000 in earnings and profits. Dog's Breath made a $100,000 interest-free loan to Augie. The loan was represented by a promissory note and was for a 10 year term, but was unsecured. The applicable Federal rate on the date the loan was made was 5%. Assume that the net present value of the $100,000 obligation, discounted at the AFR, was $61,000.

4. Kenny owns 100% of the stock of Outron Energy Corporation. Outron has millions of dollars of earnings and profits. Last year Outron sold Kenny an oil well for $1,000,000. Within days Kenny sold the oil well to a major oil company for $3,000,000. Has Outron made a dividend distribution to Kenny? What is the amount, if any, of the dividend?

5. (a) George owns 60% of the stock of the Lone Star Pharmaceutical & Brewing Corp.; the other 40% is owned by Dick, who is unrelated. In 2013, when it had accumulated earnings and profits of $1,000,000, Lone Star granted to George's daughter, Jenna, who owned no stock, an option to purchase one of its breweries for $750,000. Jenna paid $10 for the option. At that time the fair market value of the brewery was $750,000. The option was exercisable any time during the next three years. In 2015, Jenna exercised the option at a time when the value of the brewery was $1,300,000. At that time the corporation had $500,000 of earnings and profits.

(b) What if the corporation had only 200,000 of total earnings and profits in 2014?

6. Jeff owns 100% of the stock of Jeff's Reliable Used Car Corp. and Jeff's Friendly Finance, Inc. Jeff's Reliable Used Car Corp. was caught rolling back odometers and was fined $10,000 as a result of prosecution by the State. Because Jeff's Reliable Used Car Corp was short of cash, the fine was paid with a check drawn on Friendly Finance, Inc. Might there be a constructive dividend to Jeff? What additional evidence must be developed in order to be certain?

SECTION 5. INTERCORPORATE DIVIDENDS

1. Domestic Business Machines, Inc. purchased 1,000 shares of Abacus Computer Corp. in a transaction on the NASDAQ. The stock cost $100,000, and the purchase was financed by borrowing $100,000 from the Improvident Bank & Trust Co. The loan was secured by the stock.

   (a) What are the tax consequences for the current year in which Domestic Business Machines receives $4,000 of dividends on the Abacus Computer stock and pays $5,000 interest on the loan?

   (b) What if Domestic Business Machines received $10,000 of dividends?

   (c) What if Domestic Business Machines had borrowed only $60,000 of the $100,000 to purchase the stock and paid only $3,000 of interest?

   (1) Assume Domestic Business Machines received $4,000 of dividends.

   (2) Assume Domestic Business Machines received $10,000 of dividends.

   (d) What if Domestic Business Machines had borrowed $50,000,000, and purchased 80 percent of the stock of Abacus Computer? DBM received $6,000,000 of dividends and paid $5,000,000 of interest.

2. On March 15, Monolith Corporation declared a dividend of $2 per share, payable on April 1 to shareholders of record as of March 20. Close Corp. thereupon purchased 1,000 shares of Monolith common stock, which was trading on the New York Stock Exchange, for $30,000. On April 1, Close Corp. received a dividend of $2,000, and on April 5, Close Corp. sold the Monolith Corp. stock for $28,000.

   (a) What are the tax consequences to Close Corp.?

(b) How would your answer differ if Close Corp. sold the stock on December 1, instead of April 5?

(c) What is your answer if, in addition to the $2,000 dividend received on April 1, Close Corp. received another $2,000 dividend on June 1 and sold the stock on December 1?

CHAPTER 14

STOCK REDEMPTIONS

SECTION 1. INTRODUCTION

1. (a) (1) As of January 1, 2014, Julia, Charlene, Mary Jo, and Suzanne each owned 25 of the 100 outstanding shares of voting common stock of Sugerbaker's Design Corp. Suzanne's basis for her 25 shares, which she had acquired directly from the corporation for cash over ten years ago, was $80,000. Sugerbaker's had $120,000 of accumulated earnings and profits as of January 1, 2014. During 2014, Sugerbaker's had no current earnings and profits from operations. On July 1, 2014, Sugerbaker's distributed a parcel of land to Suzanne in consideration of Suzanne surrendering her 25 shares of common stock. The land had an adjusted basis to the corporation of $90,000 and a fair market value of $150,000. What are the tax consequences to Suzanne and Sugerbaker's? What are Sugerbaker's accumulated earnings and profits as of January 1, 2015?

   (2) What if Suzanne had paid the corporation $160,000 to acquire the stock from it?

   (b) Assume all of the basic facts in part (a)(1). In addition to redeeming Suzanne's 25 shares of stock, on December 31, 2014, Sugerbaker's made § 301 cash distributions of $35,000 to each of Julia, Charlene, and Mary Jo. What are the tax consequences to Julia, Charlene, Mary Jo, and Suzanne and Sugerbaker's. What are Sugerbaker's accumulated earnings and profits as of January 1, 2015?

SECTION 2. SUBSTANTIALLY DISPROPORTIONATE REDEMPTIONS

1. Champion Breakfast Drink Corp. has 100 shares of common stock and 200 shares of nonvoting preferred stock outstanding. Dwayne owns 70 shares of common stock and Kilgore owns 30 shares of common stock. Kilgore also owns 100 shares of nonvoting preferred stock. Which, if any, of the following alternative redemption transactions qualify under § 302(b)(2), and what are the tax consequences of each transaction:

(a) Champion Breakfast Drink Corp. redeems 5 shares of common stock from Kilgore for $5,000. Kilgore's basis in his 30 shares was $900 per share ($27,000 total).

(b)(1) Champion Breakfast Drink Corp. redeems 10 shares of common stock from Kilgore for $10,000. Kilgore's basis in his 30 shares of common stock was $900 per share ($27,000 total).

(2) What if Kilgore's basis in his 30 shares of common stock was $1,200 per share ($36,000 total)?

(c) Champion Breakfast Drink Corp. redeems 35 shares of common stock from Dwayne for $35,000. Dwayne's basis in his stock is $900 per share ($31,500).

(d) Champion Breakfast Drink Corp. redeems 40 shares of common stock from Dwayne for $40,000. Dwayne's basis in his stock is $900 per share ($36,000).

(e) Champion Breakfast Drink Corp. redeems 50 shares of preferred stock from Kilgore.

(f) Champion Breakfast Drink Corp. redeems 15 shares of common stock and 50 shares of preferred stock from Kilgore.

(g) Champion Breakfast Drink Corp. redeems 15 shares of common stock and 90 shares of preferred stock from Kilgore.

2. Titan Siren Corp. has 100 shares of voting common stock outstanding. Malachi owns 60 shares and Winston owns 40 shares. They have both worked full time for the corporation. On February 1, Malachi went into semi-retirement, leaving most management to Winston, and Titan Siren Corp. redeemed 30 of Malachi's shares. On August 1st, Winston died and Malachi went back to work; in December, the corporation redeemed all of Winston's shares from his estate. Does Malachi's redemption qualify under § 302(b)(2)?

3. Four years ago, Hoover's Pontiac Dealer, Inc. owned 40 shares of stock of voting common stock of Pilgrim Slaughterhouse Corp., which had 100 shares of voting common stock outstanding. Hoover's basis for the Pilgrim Slaughterhouse stock was $600 per share. Billy Pilgrim owned the other 60 shares of voting common stock. Three years ago, Pilgrim Slaughterhouse redeemed 10 shares of stock from Hoover's for $1,000 per share; two years ago Pilgrim Slaughterhouse redeemed 8 shares of stock from Hoover's for $1,000 per share; last year Pilgrim Slaughterhouse redeemed 5 shares of stock from Hoover's for $1,000 per share; this year Pilgrim Slaughterhouse redeemed 3 shares of stock

from Hoover's for $1,000 per share. What are the tax consequences to Hoover's Pontiac Dealer, Inc.?

4. Micando Corp. has 100 shares of voting common stock and 400 shares of nonvoting common stock outstanding. Each share of Micando Corp. voting common stock has a fair market value of $100. Each share of nonvoting common stock has a fair market value of $50. José owns 60 shares of Micando Corp. voting common stock and 200 shares of Micando Corp. nonvoting common stock. The remaining shares are owned by a number of unrelated individuals.

   (a) If Micando Corp. redeems 30 of José's voting common shares, will the redemption qualify for exchange treatment under 302(b)(2)?

   (b) If Micando Corp. redeems 30 of José's voting common shares, how many of José's nonvoting common shares must be redeemed to qualify the transaction under § 302(b)(2)?

5. Rosewater Corporation has 100 shares of voting common stock and 300 shares of voting preferred stock outstanding. Elliot owns 40 shares of voting common stock and 100 shares of voting preferred stock.

   (a) If Rosewater Corporation redeems all 40 of Elliot's shares of common stock, will the redemption transaction qualify under § 302(b)(2)?

   (b) If Rosewater Corporation redeems all 100 of Elliot's shares of preferred stock, will the redemption transaction qualify under § 302(b)(2)?

6. X Corporation has 100 shares of stock outstanding, all of which are owned by six related individuals, as follows:

Shareholder	Relationship	Number of Shares
Amy		25
Ben	Amy's son	15
Cindy	Ben's wife	15
David	Ben & Cindy's son	15
Evan	Amy's son	15
Fran	Evan's daughter	15

   (a) Determine how much stock is owned by each shareholder after taking into account the § 318 attribution rules.

   (b) Would a redemption of 14 shares from Ben qualify under § 302(b)(2)?

(c) Would a redemption of 14 shares from Cindy qualify under § 302(b)(2)?

(d) Would a redemption of 10 shares from Fran qualify under § 302(b)(2)?

7. Y Corp. has 100 shares of common stock outstanding. Fifteen shares are owned by A. Forty shares are owned by Z Corp., and A owns 60 of the 100 outstanding shares of stock of Z Corp. The remaining 45 shares of stock of Y Corp. are owned by the ABC Partnership, in which A is a one-third partner. Would a redemption of 10 of A's Y Corp. shares qualify under § 302(b)(2)?

8. D owns 50 percent of the stock of each of V Corporation and W Corporation. The other 50 percent of the stock of each corporation is owned by various unrelated persons. V Corporation and W Corporation each own 40 shares of common stock of Q Corporation, which has 100 shares outstanding. The other 20 shares of the stock of Q Corporation are owned by various unrelated persons. Q Corporation redeemed 21 shares of its stock (with a basis of $40,000) from W Corporation for $100,000. What are the tax consequences to W Corporation?

SECTION 3. TERMINATION OF A SHAREHOLDER'S INTEREST

1. Tony and Corrado each owned 50 shares of stock in Bada Bing Corporation. Bada Bing redeemed all 50 shares of Corrado's stock for $1,000,000 in cash. Corrado continued to work full-time for Bada Bing as public relations manager. Tony is Corrado's nephew. Does the redemption distribution qualify under § 302(b)(3)?

2. Paradise Scenic Railway Corp. has 100 shares of voting common stock outstanding. Seventy shares are owned by Henry, and thirty shares are owned by his granddaughter, Jean. Which, if any, of the following redemption transactions qualify under § 302(b)(3)?

(a) Paradise redeems all of Henry's shares for a lump sum cash payment.

(b) (1) Paradise redeems all of Henry's shares for a promissory note, payable in ten equal annual principal installments (including interest at the prime rate plus 3%), and the note is secured by a mortgage lien on all of the corporation's assets.

(2) Same as in (b)(1), but Paradise agrees that during the term of the note it will not pay any dividends, incur any indebtedness

outside the ordinary course of business, or acquire any new business, be acquired, or liquidate, without Henry's consent.

(3) Same as in (b)(1) but Henry agrees to subordinate his note to any third party lender to the corporation upon request.

(4) Paradise redeems all of Henry's shares for a promissory note, the principal of which is payable in a lump sum in ten years, with annual interest payable at the prime rate plus 3%, but if the corporation would have to borrow from a third party lender to make an interest payment the interest payment can be deferred until the due date of the principal.

3. Bassbuster Boat Corp. has 100 shares of common stock outstanding. Roland owns 60 shares and his son Orlando owns 40 shares. Roland plans to retire this year and turn complete management of the company over to Orlando. Because the corporation has inadequate retained earnings to redeem all of Roland's stock at one time and cannot borrow sufficient money to do so without incurring unreasonable business risks, the corporation will redeem 15 of Roland's shares this year and 15 shares in each of the next three years. Assuming that Roland files the § 302(c)(2) agreement, can the redemptions this year and in each of the next two years, as well as the final redemption, all qualify under § 302(b)(3)?

4. Advanced Motor Car Concepts, Inc. has two shareholders, Tucker, who owns 60 shares, and his son, Edsel, who owns 40 shares. If the corporation redeems all of Tuckers's shares and Tucker files the § 302(c)(2) agreement, will the redemption qualify under § 302(b)(3) in the following alternative circumstances.

(a) Tucker remains as an unpaid director of the corporation.

(b) The corporation promises to pay Tucker a "pension" of $20,000 for each of the next ten years. Tucker agrees not to establish any competing business and to render such consulting services as the corporation may from time to time request.

(c) Tucker is a lawyer and four years later Tucker represented the corporation in a product liability litigation matter for a contingent fee.

(d) Tucker is an engineer and five years later Tucker is hired as a consultant to help eliminate problems with the design of the company's vehicles revolutionary new engine that runs on poultry waste. Tucker's compensation was a fixed fee plus a percentage of gross sales from the first five years of sales of vehicles using the new engine.

(d)(1) Tucker owns the building in which the corporation's factory and offices are located, and Tucker had leased the building to the corporation. The lease, which has ten more years to go, calls for rent of $5,000 per month.

(2) Same as (d)(1) but contemporaneously with the redemption the lease is renegotiated to provide for rent equal to one percent of the corporation's net profits (before taking the rent into account) or $5,000, whichever is greater.

5. (a) John owned 70 out of 100 shares of the common stock of Walton's Lumber Mill Corp. John's son John-Boy owned the other 30 shares. John gave 20 shares to his grandson Jim-Bob and four months later Walton's Lumber Mill redeemed John's remaining 50 shares. Does the redemption transactions qualify under § 302(b)(3)?

   (b) John gave 40 shares to his wife, Olivia, and three months later Walton's Lumber Mill redeemed John's remaining 30 shares.

   (c) John gave 20 shares to his grandson Jim-Bob and six months later Walton's Lumber Mill redeemed Jim-Bob's 20 shares.

6. Sacramento Delta Yacht Basin, Inc. has 100 shares of common stock outstanding, all of which are owned by the Connor family. Alice owns 25 shares, her son Bob owns 25 shares, Alice's daughter Cybill owns 25 shares, and Bob's son Don owns 25 shares. Which, if any, of the following redemption transactions qualify under § 302(b)(3)?

   (a) The corporation redeems all of Alice's shares and Alice files the § 302(c)(2) agreement. Six years later Cybill dies and bequeaths her shares to Alice.

   (b) The corporation redeems all of Bob's shares and Bob files the § 302(c)(2) agreement.

   (1) Seven years later, Alice dies and bequeaths all of her shares in trust for Don, naming Bob as the trustee.

   (2) Instead of bequeathing her shares to the trust for Don, Alice established an *inter vivos* trust shortly before she died, and transferred her shares to the trust with Bob as the trustee.

7. E-Z Rider Motorcycle Manufacturing Corp. has 100 shares of common stock outstanding. Peter owns 25 shares and Jane, Peter's sister, owns 25 shares. The other 50 shares are owned by the estate of Henry. Henry was the father of Peter and Jane. Can a redemption of the 50 shares owned by Henry' estate's qualify under § 302(b)(3) by virtue of

the waiver of attribution rules under the following alternative circumstances?

(a) Frances, who is Peter's and Jane's mother, is the sole beneficiary of the estate.

(b) Frances is the residuary beneficiary of the estate, Peter and Jane each received specific cash bequests.

(c) Peter and Jane are the residuary beneficiaries of the estate.

SECTION 4. DISTRIBUTIONS NOT "ESSENTIALLY EQUIVALENT TO A DIVIDEND"

1. Blueberry E-Mail Systems, Inc. has 100 shares of common stock outstanding, which are owned as follows:

Amanda	Bill	Clarissa	Derek
28	25	24	23

In each of the following alternative situations, determine whether the redemption qualifies as not essentially equivalent to a dividend under § 302(b)(1).

(a) (1) Blueberry redeems 5 shares from Bill, who is Amanda's son. The shareholders are otherwise unrelated.

(2) Blueberry redeems 5 shares from Amanda, who is Bill's mother. Amanda, who is a graduate of Enormous State University, and Bill have not been on speaking terms since Bill refused to attend ESU and instead enrolled at Athletic State A & M University, ESU's biggest sports rival.

(b) Blueberry redeems 5 shares from Clarissa, who is Amanda's daughter. The shareholders are otherwise unrelated.

(c) Blueberry redeems 4 shares from Clarissa, who is Amanda's daughter. The shareholders are otherwise unrelated.

(d) Blueberry redeems 7 shares from Amanda. The shareholders are unrelated.

(e) Blueberry redeems 5 shares from Derek, who is Clarissa's brother. The shareholders are otherwise unrelated.

2. Organic Dairies, Inc. has 100 shares of common stock and 100 shares of nonvoting preferred stock outstanding. The preferred stock is not convertible into common stock and is not § 306 stock. Y Corp. is owned by the following unrelated shareholders.

Shareholder	Common	Preferred
Alonzo	60	10
Berta	25	55
Colin	15	15
Donna	0	20

(a) If Organic Dairies, Inc. redeems 5 preferred shares from Donna, will the redemption qualify under § 302(b)?

(b) If Organic Dairies, Inc. redeems all of its outstanding preferred stock, with respect to which shareholders will the redemption qualify under § 302(b)?

SECTION 5. PARTIAL LIQUIDATIONS

1. Griswold Corporation has one class of common stock outstanding, which is owned equally by Clark and Eddie. Each shareholder owns 1000 shares. Clarks' basis is $900,000, Eddie's basis is $12,000,000. The fair market value of each share of Griswold is $10,000. The aggregate value of the shares is $20,000,000. Griswold directly operates two distinct businesses, "Wings," an air charter business with three airplanes, and "Wally World," an amusement park. Griswold also owns all of the stock of Caddy Shack Golf Club Manufacturing, Inc., which it has held for seven years.

What are the tax consequences of the following alternative transactions?

(a)(1) Griswold sells Wally World for $4,000,000 and distributes the cash proceeds pro rata to its shareholders. Each shareholder receives $2,000,000 and surrenders 200 shares of stock. Griswold has operated Wings and Wally World for more than five years.

(2) What if each shareholder surrenders 400 shares of stock?

(3) What if neither shareholder surrenders any stock?

(b) Would your answer to the question in part (a)(1) differ if Griswold distributed only $3,000,000 to its shareholders and used the other $1,000,000 to expand the Wings business?

(c)(1) What would be the result in (a)(1) if Griswold had started the Wings business three years ago out of retained earnings?

(2) Would the answer differ if Griswold also owned 5,000 acres of undeveloped land that it purchased nine years ago as an investment, but grazing rights on the undeveloped land have been leased to a rancher for more than five years?

(3) Would the result in (a)(1) differ if Wings had been established six years ago by Joe Hacket and was purchased for cash by Griswold three years ago?

(4) Would the result in (1)(a) differ if Wings had been established six years ago by Joe Hacket and was acquired in a tax free merger of Wings into Griswold three years ago?

(d)(1) All of Griswold's businesses have been owned and operated for more than five years. The largest of Wing's several airplanes was destroyed in a hurricane and Griswold received $5,000,000 of insurance proceeds. Griswold used $2,000,000 of the insurance to buy a replacement airplane that was much smaller and carried many fewer passengers, and distributed the remaining $3,000,000 equally among its shareholders in redemption of 150 shares of stock (worth $1,500,0000) from each.

(2) Would the answer differ if Griswold distributed $4,000,000 of insurance proceeds and used the other $1,000,000 to expand the Wally World business?

(3) Would the answer in part (d)(2), above, differ if Griswold also owned 5,000 acres of undeveloped land that it purchased nine years ago as an investment?

(e) Griswold distributed pro rata 5,000 acres of undeveloped land that it purchased nine years ago as an investment, but grazing rights on the undeveloped land have been leased to a rancher for more than five years?

(f)(1) Griswold sells all of its Caddy Shack stock for $2,000,000 and distributes $1,000,000 to each shareholder in redemption of 10 shares from each.

(2) Griswold liquidates Caddy Shack, acquiring all of its assets as the sole shareholder, sells the assets for $2,000,000, and distributes $1,000,000 to each shareholder in redemption of 20 shares from each.

2. Ward owned 30 shares of Cleaver Cutlery Manufacturing Corporation, Ward's wife June owned 30 shares, and their son Theodore owned the other 40 shares. Cleaver Cutlery Manufacturing Corporation had two divisions, the kitchen cutlery division and the tableware division. Cleaver Cutlery Manufacturing Corporation sold its tableware division, and distributed the proceeds to Ward in redemption of all of his stock. June continued to hold her stock in Cleaver Cutlery Manufacturing Corporation, and Ward and June continued to serve on the board of directors. What are the tax consequences of the redemption of Ward's stock?

3. Ahab Corporation has 200 shares of common stock outstanding, which are owned equally by Jonah and Leviathan Corporation. Jonah's basis for his stock is $2,000,000; Leviathan's basis for its stock is $4,000,000. Ahab has operated two distinct businesses, a wholesale fish bait business and chain of fast-food sushi bars, for over ten years. The sushi bar business is worth $6,000,000; the wholesale fish bait business is worth $14,000,000. What are the tax consequences of the following alternative transactions?

   (a) Pursuant to a plan of partial liquidation, Ahab distributes the assets of the sushi bar business to its shareholders pro rata in redemption of 30 shares from each of them.

   (b) Pursuant to a plan of partial liquidation, Ahab distributes the assets of the sushi bar business to Leviathan Corporation in redemption of 60 of its shares.

SECTION 6. REDEMPTIONS THROUGH THE USE OF RELATED CORPORATIONS

1. Alicia owned all 100 outstanding shares of X Corp., with a basis of $60 per share. Alicia sells 60 shares of X Corp. stock to Y Corp. for $18,000 ($300 per share). Prior to the sale, X Corp. had accumulated earnings and profits of $8,000; Y Corp. had accumulated earnings and profits of $2,000 and current earnings and profits of $1,000. What are the tax consequences of the sale in the following alternative situations?

   (a) Alicia is the sole shareholder of Y Corp. Alicia's basis in the Y Corp. stock is $2,000.

   (b) Alicia is the sole shareholder of Y Corp. but Y Corp. has no current earnings and profits and a $9,000 deficit in accumulated earnings and profits.

(c) Alicia owns 40 percent of the stock of Y Corp. The remaining Y Corp. stock is owned by unrelated parties.

(d) Alicia owns no stock of Y Corp., but her daughter is the sole shareholder of Y Corp.

2. Becky owns 60 of 100 outstanding common shares of W Corp. and 50 out of 100 common shares of Z Corp. Becky sells 30 shares of W Corp., having a basis of $10,000, to Z Corp. for $50,000. W Corp. and Z Corp. each have accumulated earnings and profits of more than $50,000. What are the tax consequences to Becky?

3. Carmela owns 80 shares of the common stock of X Corp., which has 100 shares of common stock outstanding. X Corp. owns 65 shares of common stock of Y Corp., which has 100 shares outstanding. Carmela sells 35 shares of X Corp. stock to Y Corp. for $100 per share. Assume that Carmela has a basis of $25 per share in the X Corp. stock, and that X Corp. has $4,000 and Y Corp. has $6,000 of accumulated earnings and profits. What are the tax consequences to Carmela?

4. Gabrielle owned 70 out of 100 shares of common stock of Q Corporation and 30 out of 80 shares of stock of V Corporation. Gabrielle transferred 30 shares of Q Corporation stock, with a basis of $40,000, to V Corporation in exchange for 20 shares of V Corporation stock worth $50,000 and $50,000 in cash. V Corporation had over $100,000 of earnings and profits. What are the tax consequences to Gabrielle?

5. Felicity owned all of the stock of Transamerica, Inc. and Desperate Soap Corporation. Felicity's basis in the Transamerica stock was $999,999. For many years, Desperate Soap had operated separately an advertising business and a chain of day care centers. This year, Desperate Soap sold the day care center business for $1,000,000 and used the proceeds to purchase all of Felicity's Transamerica stock. Desperate Soap had over $1,000,000 of earnings and profits. What are the tax consequences to Felicity?

CHAPTER 15

STOCK DIVIDENDS

SECTION 1. TAXABLE VERSUS NONTAXABLE STOCK DIVIDEND

1. (a) X Corp. has a single class of voting common stock with 10,000 shares outstanding. The fair market value of each share is $300. If the corporation declares a dividend of one share of nonconvertible $200 par value preferred stock on each share of common stock, will the stock dividend be taxable or tax-free under § 305?

   (b) Arnie, one of the shareholders of X Corp., owns 200 shares of common stock (purchased in a single block) with a basis of $6,000. Assuming that the fair market value of the preferred stock after issuance is $100, what are the bases of Arnie's 200 shares of common and 200 shares of preferred, respectively?

2. Y Corporation has a single class of voting common stock outstanding. Y Corporation maintains a "dividend reinvestment program" by which any shareholder may elect to receive additional shares of common stock in lieu of cash dividends. If a shareholder elects to receive stock instead of cash, the stock dividend will consist of a number of whole or fractional shares having a fair market value equal to 110 percent of the dollar value of the declared cash dividend. Thus, for example, if the declared cash dividend is $1 per share at a time when shares are trading at $10 per share, a holder of 500 shares who elected to receive stock would receive 55 shares instead of a cash dividend of $500.

   (a) Are the stock dividends taxable? If so, what is the amount of the distribution?

   (b) Would the stock dividends be taxable if every shareholder elected to receive additional stock and none received cash?

3. Z Corporation has two classes of common stock, Class A and Class B. The two classes are alike in all respects except that only the Class A shares vote. Al, Beth, Chuck, and Debbie each own 200 shares of Class A voting common. Earl, Fran, George, and Helen each own 200 shares of nonvoting class B common stock. Z Corporation declared a one-on-one dividend of newly issued Class B nonvoting common stock on all common stock. Simultaneously, Z Corporation offered to redeem up to one-half of the newly issued shares received by any Class A shareholder

for $100 per share. None of the class A shareholders tendered any stock for redemption. To what extent, if any, is the stock dividend taxable?

4. X Corporation has two classes of stock outstanding, Class A voting common and Class B nonvoting $100 par value 6% preferred. X Corp. also has authorized but unissued shares of Class C nonvoting $100 par value 7% preferred.

   (a)(1) X Corporation distributes a stock dividend of newly issued Class B preferred to the Class A shareholders. Is the distribution taxable? Is whether or not X Corporation regularly paid the Class B dividend relevant?

   (2) Would your answer change if, prior to the distribution, all of both classes of stock were held by a single shareholder?

   (b) X Corporation distributes a stock dividend of newly issued Class C preferred to the Class A shareholders. The Class C preferred is junior to the Class B preferred. Is the distribution taxable?

5. Y Corporation has only a single class of voting common stock outstanding. Y Corporation also has issued a series of $1,000, 6% debt instruments convertible into common stock at the rate of ten shares of common stock for each $1,000 debt instrument. Y Corporation declared a two-for-one stock split, distributing to each shareholder newly issued shares equal in number to the shares previously held. Must the conversion ratio on the debt instruments be increased to avoid a taxable stock dividend?

6. Z Corporation has outstanding Class A voting common stock and Class B participating preferred stock. Class B is entitled to a noncumulative preferred dividend of $1 per share if cash dividends are declared, and a liquidation preference of $100 per share. After the preference is satisfied, Class A and Class B share dividends and liquidation proceeds in a 60 percent to 40 percent ratio. Z Corporation declared a stock dividend of one share of Class A stock on each share of Class A stock and one share of Class B stock on each share of Class B stock. Is the distribution taxable?

7. X Corporation has outstanding Class A voting common stock and Class B nonvoting convertible preferred stock. The Class B stock is convertible into Class A at the ratio of ten shares of Class A for each share of Class B. X Corporation pays regular dividends on the Class B preferred stock.

(a) X Corporation declares a one-for-one stock dividend on the Class A common stock and the conversion ratio for the Class B stock is increased to 20 to 1. Is there a taxable stock dividend?

(b) Would there be a taxable stock dividend if the ratio at which Class B was convertible into Class A stock were adjusted to 21 to 1?

(c) Would there be a taxable stock dividend if the ratio at which Class B was convertible into Class A stock were adjusted to 19 to 1?

8. Y Corporation has outstanding a single class of voting common stock. The corporation declared a dividend on the common of newly issued convertible preferred stock. The preferred stock is convertible into common stock at any time in the next 20 years at a price equal to 110 percent of the common stock's market price on the date of the distribution of the convertible preferred. Is the stock dividend taxable?

9. W Corporation, the common stock of which is publicly traded, proposes to distribute as a pro rata stock dividend on its common stock newly issued $100 par value, 10% Class B nonvoting convertible preferred stock. The preferred stock will be callable by W Corporation after ten years at $120, and, if it is not called, it becomes convertible into W Corporation common stock at a price equal to 50 percent of the then current trading price of the common stock. How will the preferred stock be treated if it is issued?

10. Z Corporation's stock is publicly traded. If Z Corporation purchases ten percent of its outstanding common stock on the open market, for the purpose of enhancing the value of the shares remaining outstanding, have the holders of the remaining stock received a taxable stock dividend?

11. X Corporation has one class of outstanding common stock, which is held by unrelated individuals D (500 shares), E (300 shares) and F (200 shares). Will § 305(c) create a constructive stock dividend if X Corporation agrees to redeem annually 50 shares of stock at the election of each shareholder, and D makes such an election for two consecutive years?

SECTION 2. THE PREFERRED STOCK BAILOUT

1. Tacoma Grace Urgent Treatment Centers, Inc. is owned by five shareholders who each own 1,000 shares of the common stock. Until 2011 Tacoma Grace had only one class of stock outstanding. In 2011, Tacoma Grace declared a dividend of 1 share of $1,000 par value 7% voting preferred stock for every ten shares of common then held by its

shareholders. Each shareholder received 100 shares of preferred stock. Immediately after the distribution, the fair market value of each share of preferred stock was $1,000 and the fair market value of each share of common stock was $50. Tacoma Grace had no current earnings and profits in 2011, but it had accumulated earnings and profits of $295,000. Tacoma Grace made no other distributions in 2011.

(a)(1) In 2014, when Tacoma Grace had current earnings and profits of $200,000 and accumulated earnings and profits from prior years of $300,000, one shareholder, Dr. Burke, who originally had an adjusted basis of $45,000 in his Tacoma Grace common stock, sold his 100 shares of preferred stock to another shareholder for $100,000 ($1,000 per share). What are the tax consequences of the sale?

(2) Would your answer change if in 2014 Tacoma Grace had no current earnings and profits and only $10,000 of accumulated earnings and profits?

(3) Would your answer differ if in 2011, when the stock dividend was distributed, Tacoma Grace had $1,000,000 of accumulated earnings and profits?

(4) What if Dr. Burke sold 500 shares of his common stock and 50 shares of his preferred stock to Dr. Grey, who previously owned no shares in Tacoma Grace?

(5) Would your answer to (a)(1) differ if the preferred stock were participating preferred stock, which after its preference shared dividend and liquidation rights with the common stock in a nine-to-one ratio?

(6) What if Dr. Burke gave his preferred stock to his niece, who then sold the stock to the Rock of Ages Insurance Co.?

(7) What if Dr. Burke died and bequeathed all of his common and preferred stock to his niece, who kept the common stock but sold the preferred stock to the Rock of Ages Insurance Co.?

(b)(1) In 2014, when Tacoma Grace had current earnings and profits of $200,000 and accumulated earnings and profits from prior years of $300,000, Tacoma Grace redeemed from Dr. Webber, another Tacoma Grace shareholder, all 100 of his preferred shares for $100,000. Dr. Webber originally had an adjusted basis of $90,000 in his Tacoma Grace common stock.

(2) Would your answer change if in 2014 Tacoma Grace had no current earnings and profits and only $10,000 of accumulated earnings and profits?

(3) What if Dr. Webber retired and Tacoma Grace redeemed all of his common and preferred stock at the same time?

CHAPTER 16

CORPORATE LIQUIDATIONS

SECTION 2. TREATMENT OF THE CORPORATION

SECTION 3. TREATMENT OF SHAREHOLDERS

1. Wilbur owns 600 of 1,000 outstanding shares of Dayton Airplane and Bicycle Corporation. Wilbur acquired 400 shares for $50,000 approximately 20 years ago and 200 shares late last year for $1,900,000. What are the tax consequences to Wilbur on the liquidation of Dayton Corporation in the following alternative situations?

   (a) Dayton sells its assets for cash, after which it has aggregate current and accumulated earnings and profits of $7,400,000. After paying all its debts, Dayton distributes $6,000,000 to Wilbur in complete liquidation.

   (b) Dayton sells its assets for cash, after which it has a deficit in earnings and profits. Dayton distributes $300,000 to Wilbur in complete liquidation.

   (c) Dayton was unable to find a single purchaser for all of its assets. It sold some of its assets last year and distributed $3,000,000 to Wilbur last year. This year, after selling its remaining assets and paying its debts, it distributes $1,500,000 to Wilbur. Is the date of adoption of a formal plan of liquidation crucial? Does the nature of the assets sold last year have any bearing on whether the adoption of a formal plan of liquidation is important?

   (d) Assume that Wilbur acquired all 600 shares at the same time for $2,000,000. Dayton sells it assets and distributes to Wilbur in complete liquidation $4,500,000 of cash and a promissory note from Armstrong Corp., which purchased some of the Dayton assets, with a principal amount of $1,500,000, due in five years, with interest payable semi-annually at the prime rate plus 3%.

      (1) What if the promissory note was received by Dayton two years ago in exchange for a bicycle factory building, which had an adjusted basis of $300,000?

(2) What if the promissory note was received by Dayton eleven months ago, after Dayton had adopted a resolution to liquidate, in exchange for a bicycle factory, which had an adjusted basis of $300,000?

(3) What if the promissory note was received by Dayton eleven months ago, after Dayton had adopted a resolution to liquidate, in exchange for all its inventory, which had an adjusted basis of $300,000?

(4) What if the promissory note was received by Dayton eleven months ago, after Dayton had adopted a resolution to liquidate, in exchange for its bicycle inventory, which had an adjusted basis of $300,000. Dayton's remaining inventory was sold to other purchasers?

2. Steve owned 500 shares of stock of Florida Gator Farms, Inc. His basis for the stock was $1,000,000. Florida Gator Farms, Inc. liquidated, and in the process, after the corporation paid all of its debts (other than mortgages encumbering distributed real estate), reserving enough cash to pay its tax liability for the year, it distributed to Steve $2,000,000 of cash and Swampacre, a parcel of real estate previously used in its trade or business. Florida Gator's adjusted basis for Swampacre was $3,000,000. Its fair market value was $10,000,000.

   (a) How much gain or loss must be recognized by Florida Gator Farms and by Steve?

   (b) How much gain or loss must be recognized by Florida Gator Farms and by Steve if Swampacre is subject to a mortgage of $4,000,000 that Steve assumes? What is the character of the corporation's gain? What is Steve's basis in the property after it is distributed?

   (c) Would your answer differ if the mortgage was a nonrecourse mortgage and Steve merely took the property subject to the mortgage rather than assuming the mortgage?

   (d) How would your answers in parts (a) and (b) differ if the amount of the mortgage were $11,000,000?

3. Joe is the sole shareholder of Milagro Bean Corporation. His basis for the stock is $200,000. The sole asset of Milagro Bean Corporation is a parcel of farm land.

   (a) The corporation's adjusted basis for the land is $300,000. The fair market value of the land is $300,000. How much gain or loss must be recognized by Milagro Bean Corporation and by Joe if the corporation distributes the property to Joe subject to a mortgage of $300,000? What is Joe's basis in the property after it is distributed?

(b) How would your answer differ if the corporation's adjusted basis for the land was $320,000 and the amount of the mortgage was $315,000?

(c) How would your answer differ if the corporation's adjusted basis for the land was $200,000 and the amount of the mortgage was $300,000?

4. The outstanding stock of the Bassamatic Corporation is owned by Julia, who owns 60 shares, and Mario, who owns 40 shares. Bassamatic's assets available for distribution after paying all of its debts, including taxes for the year of the liquidation, are as follows:

Asset	Adj. Basis	F.M.V.
Factory	$100,000	$300,000
Equipment	$300,000	$200,000
Inventory	$100,000	$200,000
Cash	$300,000	$300,000

On January 1 of the current year, Bassamatic adopted a plan of complete liquidation. What are the tax consequences to Bassamatic of each of the following alternative distributions?

(a)(1) Bassamatic distributes its assets pro rata to Julia and Mario, who will thereafter operate the business as 60/40 partners.

(2) Bassamatic transfers all of the assets to the newly formed Pasta Magic LLC in exchange for all 10 membership units of the LLC, immediately after which Bassamatic liquidates by distributing 6 Pasta Magic LLC units to Julia and 4 Pasta Magic LLC units to Mario.

(b) Bassamatic distributes the Factory, Inventory, and $100,000 of cash to Julia and the Equipment and $200,000 of Cash to Mario.

(c) Bassamatic distributes the Factory, Equipment, and $100,00 of cash to Julia, and the Inventory and $200,000 of cash to Mario.

5. Shrub Game Farm and Real Estate Development Corp. has 100 shares of common stock outstanding. George owns 80 shares and Dick owns 20 shares. Shrub owns two parcels of land, Carlsbad and Teton, and has $200,000 in cash. Both properties have been operated as game farm hunting reserves, where well-healed lawyers and lobbyists could entertain politicians (for a price, of course). The basis and fair market values of the properties are as follows:

Asset	Adj. Basis	F.M.V.
Carlsbad	$400,000	$600,000
Teton	$500,000	$200,000

What are the tax consequences to the corporation of the following alternative liquidating distributions?

(a) Shrub distributes its assets to George and Dick as tenants in common, George taking an undivided 4/5ths in each parcel of real estate (and $160,000 in cash) and Dick taking an undivided 1/5th in each parcel of land (and $40,000 in cash). Teton was acquired four years ago, when its fair market value and basis were both $500,000, as a contribution by George in a § 351 transaction in exchange for enough stock to increase his stock ownership from 40 percent to 80 percent.

(b)(1) Shrub sells Carlsbad for $600,000 and Teton for $200,000 and distributes $800,000 in cash to George and $200,000 in cash to Dick. Carlsbad had been held for six years, but Teton, and another property, Old Faithful (which was sold last year), were contributed by George eighteen months ago in exchange for stock in a § 351 transaction. Teton's fair market fair market value at that time was $380,000 and its adjusted basis was $500,000. Old Faithful's fair market fair market value at that time was $200,000 and its adjusted basis was $80,000. Both Carlsbad and Teton were operated as hunting reserves and the primary customers were well-healed lawyers and lobbyists who paid the corporation to use the facilities to entertain politicians.

(2) What if Teton was land held for speculative investment and no business was conducted on the property?

(3) What if Teton was held for speculative investment and Shrub had no plans to develop it, and it was contributed two and one-half years ago?

6. Jordan and Garret each own 50 shares of stock of Cavanaugh & Macy, P.S.C., which operates a pathology laboratory. Each of them has a basis of $20,000 in their stock. The corporation has over 20 employees. The corporation's tangible assets consist of equipment with a fair market value of $50,000 and a basis of $15,000. It operates its business in leased premises. Because of the good reputation of the business and its large customer base, a much larger medical laboratory corporation, Frankenstein, Inc. recently offered to purchase the business for $1,000,000. Jordan and Garret declined the offer. Jordan and Garret are now considering liquidating the corporation and continuing the business as a partnership. What are the tax consequences?

7. Dill is the sole shareholder of Pastel Pill Corporation. Pastel Pill's sole asset is a patent on a pharmaceutical product that has been licensed to Miracle Drugs, Inc. for manufacturing and marketing. The terms of the license call for Miracle to pay Pastel Pill 5 percent of gross sales from the drug. Miracle has not yet started marketing the drug, but plans to do so starting next year. Sales are estimated to be anywhere between $6,000,000 and $100,000,000 a year for at least six to ten years. As a result, over that period royalties might total as little as $300,000 or as much as $5,000,000. What are the tax consequences of liquidating Pastel Pill Corporation?

SECTION 4. LIQUIDATION OF SUBSIDIARY CORPORATIONS – SECTION 332

1. Global Automotive Corp. owns 80 shares of the 100 outstanding shares of common stock of Specific Motors Corp. The remaining 20 shares of the Specific Motors stock are owned by Tucker Vehicles, Inc. Global's basis for its shares is $8,000,000; Tucker's basis is $2,000,000. Specific Motor's assets consist of an automobile factory, with a fair market value of $20,000,000 and a basis of $9,000,000 and 100 shares of stock in Adobe Motors Corp., with a fair market value of $5,000,000 and a basis of $4,000,000. Both assets have been held for more than 5 years.

   (a) If Specific Motors liquidates and distributes the factory to Global and the Adobe Motors stock to Tucker, what are the tax consequences to Specific Motors, Global, and Tucker?

   (b) How would your answer to (a) differ if Global's basis for the Specific Motors stock was $30,000,000?

   (c) How would your answer to (a) differ if Specific Motor's basis for the factory was $30,000,000 and its basis for the Adobe stock was $6,000,000?

   (d)(1) How would your answer to (a) differ if Global's 80 shares of common stock was 100% of the common stock and Tucker's 20 shares was preferred stock?

   (2) What if Tucker's 20 shares of Global was participating preferred stock?

2. Psi Airlines Corp. owns all 100 outstanding shares of common stock of Southland Commuter AirLink, Inc. Its basis in the 100 shares of common stock is $6,000,000 and the fair market value of the common stock is $5,000,000. Southland's assets consist of four airplanes, each with an adjusted basis of $600,000 and a fair market value of

$700,000, and terminal facilities at several airports with an aggregate basis of $800,000 and a fair market value of $1,000,000, and licenses and landing rights with a basis of $2,000,000 and a fair market value of $1,200,000.

(a) Could Psi and Southland recognize their loss if Psi sold 21 shares of its common stock in Southland to National Airlines prior to voting on a plan of liquidation?

(b) Could Psi and Southland recognize their loss if Psi sold 21 shares of its common stock in Southland to National Airlines after voting on a plan of liquidation?

(c) Could Psi recognize its loss if Southland issued 1,000 shares of $1,000 par value voting preferred stock to an investment banking firm for cash before voting on a plan of liquidation?

(d) Could Psi recognize its loss if Southland adopted a liquidation resolution and then distributed one airplane this year, and another airplane on December 31st of each of the next three years, and the terminal facilities and landing rights on January 1st following the distribution of the last airplane?

3. Sunny Entertainment Corporation owns 75 percent of the stock of Rock-Around-the-Clock Compact Disk Mfg. Company. Motown Recording Company owns the other 25 percent of the Rock-Around-the-Clock stock. The assets of Rock-Around-the-Clock are worth $20,000,000. Sunny' basis in the stock of Rock-Around-the-Clock is $6,000,000 and the fair market value of the stock is $15,000,000. Sunny plans to liquidate Rock-Around-the-Clock and has asked your opinion regarding whether either or both of the following plans would work permit Sunny to avoid recognizing its gain with respect to its stock in Rock-Around-the-Clock.

   (a) Prior to holding a vote to liquidate Rock-Around-the-Clock, Sunny would purchase all of the stock owned by Motown for $5,000,000 (thereby receiving $20,000,000 in the liquidating distribution as a result of owning all the stock).

   (b) Prior to holding a vote to liquidate Rock-Around-the-Clock, Sunny would cause Rock-Around-the-Clock redeem all of the stock owned by Motown for $5,000,000 (thereby resulting in Sunny receiving $15,000,000 in the liquidation).

4. Salad Chopper, Inc. owns all of the stock of Bassamatic Corporation. Bassamatic is capitalized with (1) 200 shares of common stock, (2) 2,000 shares of $1,000 par value preferred stock, with an aggregate

liquidation preference of $2,000,000, and (3) a $3,000,000 promissory note held by Salad Chopper. Salad Chopper's basis in the common stock of Bassamatic is $4,000,000, its basis in the preferred stock is $2,000,000, and its basis in the debt is $3,000,000. What are the tax consequences to Salad Chopper of the liquidation of Bassamatic in the following alternative circumstances?

(a) Bassamatic's assets have a fair market value of $5,100,000 and a basis of $8,000,000.

(b) Bassamatic's assets have a fair market value of $4,900,000 and a basis of $8,000,000.

(c) Bassamatic's assets have a fair market value of $4,900,000 and a basis of $1,000,000.

(d) Bassamatic's assets have a fair market value of $3,000,000 and a basis of $1,000,000.

5. VideoGiant Corporation owns all of the common stock of Cathode Tube Manufacturing Corporation. VideoGiant's basis in the stock is $10,000,000. Cathode Tube owes VideoGiant $1,000,000 on a five year, 10% promissory note issued in connection with an infusion of working capital to Cathode Tube two years ago. Cathode Tube's assets consist of a factory with a fair market value of $10,000,000 and a basis of $6,000,000 and a patent with a fair market value of $1,000,000 and a basis of $4,000,000. What are the tax consequences if Cathode Tube liquidates by transferring the patent to VideoGiant in payment of the promissory note and transferring the factory in cancellation of the stock?

PART III

ELECTIVE PASSTHROUGH TAX TREATMENT

CHAPTER 17

S CORPORATIONS

SECTION 2. ELIGIBILITY, ELECTION AND TERMINATION

A. SHAREHOLDER RULES

1. Would X Corp., a domestic corporation, qualify to make a valid Subchapter S election under the following alternative situations?

   (a) X Corp. has 101 individual shareholders all of whom are unrelated except that two of them are husband and wife.

   (b) X Corp. has 101 individual shareholders, all of whom are unrelated, except for Alberto and Beryl, who are parent and child.

   (c) (1) X Corp. has 101 unrelated individual shareholders except that two of whom are remote cousins whose grandmothers were sisters.

(2) X Corp. has 150,000 shareholders, each one of which belongs to one of 99 different families, within which each family member/shareholder can trace ancestry to a single great-great-great-great grandparent.

(3) X Corp. has 101 shareholders, all of whom are related only through a single common great-great-great-great-great grandparent.

(d)(1) X Corp. has one shareholder of record, Debby, a U.S. citizen, who is married to Ernesto, a Mexican citizen, and the stock was issued while they were married. Debby and Ernesto live in Santa Fe, New Mexico.

(2) What if Debby and Ernesto live in Mexico City, Mexico?

(3) What if Debby is married to Eddie, a Canadian citizen, and they live in Vancouver, Canada?

(e) X Corp. has 10 equal shareholders. Nine of the shareholders are individual U.S. citizens. The tenth shareholder is a general partnership, the partners of which are two individual U.S. citizens.

2. Y Corp. has five shareholders, A, B, C, D, and E. It made a valid Subchapter S election effective for a prior year. Would it be eligible to keep its election in effect under the following alternative circumstances?

(a) Three years ago, A died and his estate held the shares for two years. This year, the estate terminated and distributed A's shares to a trust. Under the terms of the trust, A's surviving spouse, G, is entitled to the trust income for life, and upon G's death the corpus of the trust is to be distributed to A's descendants per capita.

(b) This year, B transferred her shares to a revocable trust with income to be distributed in the trustee's discretion among B's three children until the death of the last child, when the remainder will be distributed to B's descendants per capita.

(c) This year, C transferred his shares to an irrevocable inter vivos trust, under the terms of which C's child, H, is entitled to the trust income for life, and upon H's death, the income is to be distributed in the trustee's discretion between H's children, I and J for their lives, and, upon the death of the last of them to die, the corpus of the trust is to be distributed to C's descendants per capita.

(d) This year, D and E transferred their shares to a voting trust, naming L as the trustee. L has the power to vote the shares, receive distributions, and remit the distributions to D and E.

B. CORPORATE ELIGIBILITY

1. A, B, and C, all of whom are resident individuals, are planning to form Z Corp. Assuming that Z Corp. otherwise will qualify to make an S election, will the following alternative capital structures affect the Z Corp.'s eligibility?

   (a) A and B each will receive 100 shares of voting common stock. C will receive 100 shares of nonvoting preferred stock.

   (b) A and B each will receive 100 shares of voting common stock. C will receive 100 shares of nonvoting common stock.

   (c) A and B each will receive 100 shares of voting common stock. C will receive 100 shares of voting preferred stock.

   (d) A, B and C each will receive 100 shares of voting common stock. C, who will receive the stock for services (unlike A and B, who are contributing cash), has signed a shareholders' agreement providing that she may not transfer her shares without the consent of A and B, but if they do not consent they must purchase C's shares at book value. A and B are not subject to any restrictions on transfer.

   (e) A, B, and C each will receive 100 shares of voting common stock. To attract D, who will be a key employee, Z Corp. will issue to D an option to acquire 100 shares at 80% of the then current fair market value.

2. E, F, and G, all of whom are resident individuals, are planning to form Q Corp. E, F, and G each will receive 100 shares of voting common stock. Assuming that Q Corp. otherwise will qualify to make an S election, will the following alternative capital structures affect Q Corp.'s eligibility?

   (a)(1) E will lend Q Corp. $600,000 and receive a promissory note due in 30 years, with interest payable annually at the prime rate plus 4%.

   (2) What if E's note is subordinated to all third party creditors, including trade creditors?

   (3) What if the promissory note E receives is convertible into Q Corp. common stock based on a price estimated to be 110 percent of the

fair market value of the Q Corp. common stock on the date the note was issued?

(b) E, F and G each will lend Q Corp. $200,000 and receive a convertible promissory note due in 30 years, with interest payable annually at the prime rate plus 3%. The notes are convertible into Q Corp. common stock based on a price estimated to be 90 percent of the fair market value of the Q Corp. common stock on the date the note was issued.

(c)(1) The Stallmuckers Federal Credit Union will lend Q Corp. $600,000 and receive a promissory note due in 30 years, with interest payable annually at the prime rate plus 5 percentage points.

(2) The Stallmuckers Federal Credit Union will lend Q Corp. $600,000 and receive a promissory note due in 30 years, with interest payable annually at the prime rate plus 5 percent of Q Corp.'s net profits.

C. S CORPORATION ELECTION PROCEDURES

1. (a) X Corp. was formed on March 1 of the current year by A, B, and C, all of whom are resident individuals.

(1) By what date must X Corp. make an election if it wants to be an S Corporation?

(2) How is the election made? What if A, B, and C are married individuals, and A lives in California, which is a community property state, but B and C live in Florida, which is a common law property state?

(3) If a valid election was made on March 5th of the current year, what would be the effect of C selling her shares to D on May 15th.

(b) Y Corp. has been in existence for several years. Its stock has been owned by D and E, resident individuals, and F a nonresident alien. On February 1, of this year, D and E each purchased one-half of F's stock. Can Y Corp. elect to be an S corporation for this year? By when must it make an election if it wants to be an S corporation for next year?

D. REVOCATION OR TERMINATION OF S CORPORATION STATUS

1. Z Corp. has had a valid S election in effect for several years. G owns 40 percent of the stock; each of H, I, J, and K own 15 percent.

(a) How can Z Corp. revoke its S election for the current year?

(b) How can Z Corp. revoke its S election for the subsequent year?

(c) If Z Corp. revokes its election for the current year, when can Z Corp. make a new effective subchapter S election?

(d) Suppose that in (b), the revocation was filed on July 1 of this year, to be effective as of January 1 of next year, but that on September 3 of this year, G, H, I, and J decide they want to revoke the termination election. K does not want to revoke the termination election. Can the termination election be revoked?

2. H transferred her shares to a spray trust for her minor children. The financial planner and accountant who advised H assured her that the trust was an eligible shareholder, but in fact it is not. Is there any way that Z Corp.'s S election can be preserved without interruption?

3. I wants to revoke the election, but none of the other shareholders want to revoke the election. With the intention of terminating Z Corp. S status, I transfers one of his shares to Inc. Corp., his wholly owned corporation. Has I succeeded in terminating the election?

SECTION 3. EFFECT OF THE SUBCHAPTER S ELECTION BY A CORPORATION WITH NO C CORPORATION HISTORY

A. PASSTHROUGH OF INCOME AND LOSS

(1) GENERAL PRINCIPLES

1. Cyclone Video Corp. elected S corporation status for its first year of operation. Cyclone Video Corp.'s common stock is owned by Andrea (100 shares with a $20,000 basis) and Barry (50 shares with a $22,000 basis). Cyclone Video Corp.'s operating income is derived primarily from movie and video game DVD rentals. During the current year, Cyclone Video Corp. had the following income and expense items:

Income	
DVD rental receipts	$198,000
Tax-exempt interest	$ 6,000
Gain from the sale of a building (§ 1231 gain)	$ 36,000
STCG from the sale of publicly traded stock	$ 30,000
Expenditures and Losses	
Salaries	$62,000
Equipment expenses deducted under § 179	$15,000
Depreciation	$ 9,000

Rent	$40,000
Interest expense (on loan to purchase DVDs)	$12,000
LTCL from the sale of investment real estate	$18,000
Lobbying expenses re: anti-pornography legislation	$12,000

(a) How should Cyclone Video Corp., Andrea, and Barry report these items?
(b) What will be Andrea's and Barry's bases in their Cyclone Video Corp. stock at the end of the current year?

2. The stock of Hurricane Hardware & Lumber Co., Inc., which has had a valid S election in effect at all times, is owned equally by Chantal and Dean, each of whom had a $6,000 basis in the stock as of January 1 of last year. On July 1 of last year, Chantal lent $7,000 to Hurricane Hardware & Lumber Co. and received a 6% demand note from the corporation.

   (a)(1) What are the consequences to Chantal and Dean if Hurricane Hardware & Lumber Co. has a $20,000 loss from business operations last year?

   (2) Would your answer differ if on December 30 of last year, Hurricane Hardware & Lumber Co. repaid Chantal $4,000 of the $7,000 owed on the promissory note?

   (b)(1) If after losing $20,000 last year, Hurricane Hardware & Lumber Co. realizes $12,000 of net income from business operations in this year, what are the consequences to Chantal and Dean? Assume that the $7,000 debt from the corporation to Chantal remains outstanding.

   (2) Would your answer differ if during this year Hurricane Hardware & Lumber Co. distributed $6,000 to each shareholder?

   (c) What would be the result in (a)(1) if Hurricane Hardware & Lumber's S corporation status terminated as of January 1, 2007.

3. As of January 1 of the current year, Erin and Felix each owned one-half of the 100 outstanding shares of Tropical Wave Rider Mfg. Corp., which has had a valid S election in effect since its incorporation. During the current year, Tropical Wave had $360,000 of net income from business operations. Net operating income of $90,000 was realized in January through June, and net operating income of $270,000 was realized in July through December. In addition, in March, Tropical Wave sold an item of § 1231 property and recognized a $120,000 loss. Tropical Wave made no distributions during the current year. At the beginning of the

current year, Erin's basis in her stock was $140,000. On June 30, Erin sold 25 of her 50 shares to Gabrielle for $180,000.

(a) What are the consequences to Erin and Gabrielle if no election is made to "close the books" under Treas. Reg. § 1.1368-1(g)?

(b) What are the consequences to Erin and Gabrielle if an election is made to "close the books" under Treas. Reg. § 1.1368-1(g)?

4. Helene and Isaac each owned one-half of the 100 outstanding shares of Miami Windmill Mfg. Corp., which had a valid S election in effect since from the time of its incorporation until July of the current year. As of July 1, Miami Windmill's S election was terminated. From January through June, Miami Windmill had earned $500,000 in income and had $200,000 of deductions. As of December 31, Miami Windmill had $2,000,000 of income and $600,000 of deductions for the year. How must the parties account for the income and deductions?

(2) EFFECT OF INDIRECT CONTRIBUTIONS ON LIMITATION OF LOSS DEDUCTIONS TO SHAREHOLDERS BASIS

1. The stock of Gale Force Wind Anemometer and Barometer Mfg. Corp., which has had a valid S election in effect at all times, is owned equally by Humberto and Ingrid, each of whom had $20,000 basis in the stock as of January 1 of the current year. For the current year, Gale Force realized a $70,000 operating loss and had no other relevant tax items. To what extent may each of Humberto and Ingrid deduct their $35,000 share of the loss under the following circumstances?

(a) On December 31, the Last National Bank of Key West lent Gale Force $60,000 and both Humberto and Ingrid guaranteed repayment of the full amount of the loan if Gale Force defaulted. Humberto and Ingrid each gave the bank a mortgage on their personal residences to secure the guarantee.

(b) (1) On December 31, the Last National bank of Key West lent each of Humberto and Ingrid $30,000, at the prime rate, due in two years. Humberto and Ingrid in turn each lent the $30,000 to Gale force at the prime rate, due in two years.

(2) Would your answer be affected if Gale Force guaranteed repayment of the full amount of the loans by the bank to Humberto and Ingrid if they defaulted and Gale Force gave the bank a mortgage on its factory to secure the guarantee?

B. DISTRIBUTIONS

1. Saffir & Simpson Weathervane Mfg. Corp. has had a valid S election in effect at all times since its incorporation. The Saffir & Simpson stock is owned one-third by Arthur and two-thirds by Bertha. At the beginning of the current year, Arthur's basis in his shares was $6,000 and Bertha's basis in her shares was $2,000. During the current year, Saffir & Simpson earned $36,000 of net income from operations. Arthur's share was $12,000; Bertha's share was $24,000. What are the results to Saffir & Simpson Corp., Arthur, and Bertha in the following alternative situations?

   (a) On July 1st, Saffir & Simpson distributed $16,000 to Arthur and $32,000 to Bertha.

   (b) On December 31st, Saffir & Simpson distributed Blackacre, having a fair market value of $12,000 and a basis of $8,000, to Arthur and Whiteacre, having a fair market value of $24,000 and a basis of $22,000, to Bertha.

   (c) On December 31st, Saffir & Simpson distributed $18,000 in cash to Arthur and distributed Greenacre, which had a fair market value of $36,000 and a basis of $42,000, to Bertha.

2. Thunderbird Auto Rentals Corp. has been an S corporation since it was formed. Thelma owns 60 percent and Louise owns 40 percent of the stock of Thunderbird Auto Rentals. Thelma's basis for her stock as of December 31st of last year was $280,000; Louise's basis for her stock as of December 31st was $220,000. On January 1st of the current year, Thunderbird Auto Rentals liquidated by distributing Blackacre to Thelma and Whiteacre to Louise. These properties were purchased four years ago. The fair market value of Blackacre was $1,200,000 and Thunderbird Corp.'s basis in Blackacre was $200,000. The fair market value of Whiteacre was $1,100,000 and its basis was $1,400,000; Whiteacre was subject to a $300,000 mortgage, which Louise assumed. What are the tax consequences of the liquidation of Thunderbird Auto Rentals?

3. San Francisco Ice Pick Mfg. Corporation has had an S election in effect since it was formed in 1987. Catherine owns 60 shares of the stock of San Francisco Ice Pick Mfg. Corporation, and Nick owns 40 shares. Catherine's basis for the 60 shares is $180,000. On December 31st of this year, San Francisco Ice Pick Mfg. Corporation distributes $150,000 in cash to Catherine in redemption of 20 of Catherine's shares. What are the tax consequences to Catherine?

4. Z Corp. has had an S election in effect for all relevant times. G owns one-third of the stock of Z Corp; H owns two-thirds of the stock. Both

are employed full time by Z Corp. and each receives a salary of $30,000. Z Corp. pays $3,000 for medical insurance for each of G and H in their capacity as employees. During the current year, Z Corp. earned $90,000 of net profits before taking the salaries and medical insurance premiums with respect to G and H into account. What are the tax consequences to G and H?

SECTION 4. QUALIFED SUBCHAPTER S SUBSIDIARIES

1. (a) X Corp., which is owned by five resident individuals, owns 100 percent of the voting common stock of Y Corp., which is the only Y Corp. stock outstanding.

   (1) May X or Y make an S election?

   (2) May a Q-Sub election be made with respect to Y Corp.? Who makes the election?

   (b) X Corp., which is owned by five resident individuals, owns 99 percent of the voting common stock of Y Corp. The other 1 percent of Y Corp.'s voting common stock is owned by the X Corp. shareholders in the same proportion in which they own the X Corp. stock. May a Q-Sub election be made with respect to Y Corp.?

   (c) X Corp. owns 100 percent of the voting common stock of Z Corp. and D, who is unrelated to X Corp. or any of its shareholders, owns 100 percent of the nonvoting preferred stock of Z Corp. May a Q-Sub election be made with respect to Z Corp.?

2. Leviathan Recording Corp., which has a valid S election in effect, owns all of the stock of E-Tunes, Inc., which currently is a C Corporation. Leviathan's basis in the stock of E-Tunes is $1,000,000. What are the tax consequences of making a Q-Sub election for E-Tunes under the following alternative fact patterns?

   (a) E-Tunes's assets have a basis of $900,000 and fair market value of $2,000,000, and E-Tunes is debt free.

   (b) E-Tunes's assets have a basis of $900,000 and fair market value of $2,000,000, and E-Tunes owes $2,100,000 to the BigOne National Bank.

3. Fox Book Stores Corp., which has a valid S election in effect, owns all of the stock of The Shop Around the Corner, Inc., for which a valid Q-Sub election is in effect. Leviathan's original basis in the stock of The Shop Around the Corner, before the Q-Sub election was made in a prior year,

was $1,000,000. What are the tax consequences of revoking The Shop Around the Corner's Q-Sub election under the following alternative fact patterns?

(a) The Shop Around the Corner's assets have a basis of $900,000 and fair market value of $2,000,000, and The Shop Around the Corner is debt free.

(b) The Shop Around the Corner's assets have a basis of $900,000 and fair market value of $2,000,000. The Shop Around the Corner owes $1,500,000 to the BigOne National Bank

SECTION 5. S CORPORATIONS THAT HAVE A C CORPORATION HISTORY

A. DISTRIBUTIONS FROM AN S CORPORATION WITH EARNINGS AND PROFITS ACCUMULATED FROM SUBCHAPTER C YEARS

1. Ariel Corp. was formed seven years ago by John, who owns one-third of the stock, and Max, who owns two-thirds of the stock. Ariel Corp. did not elect S corporation status until January 1st of the current year As of December 31st of last year Ariel Corp. had $12,000 of accumulated earnings and profits. On January 1st of the current year, John had a $2,000 basis in his stock and Max had a $14,000 basis in his stock. For the current year, Ariel Corp. has $36,000 of taxable income from business operations. What are the tax consequences to Ariel Corp., John and Max in the following alternative situations?

   (a) In April of the current year, Ariel Corp. distributes $20,000 to John and in November, Ariel Corp. distributes $40,000 to Max.

   (b) During the current year, Ariel Corp. made no distributions. Ariel Corp. validly revoked its election effective January 1, of next year. Next year Ariel Corp. has $10,000 of earnings and profits. On August 1st of next year, X Corp. distributes $12,000 to John and $24,000 to Max.

B. PASSIVE INVESTMENT INCOME OF AN S CORPORATION WITH ACCUMULATED EARNINGS AND PROFITS

1. For the current taxable year, Y Corp., which is wholly owned by A, and which has a valid S corporation election, has substantial earnings and profits from its C corporation history. It has gross receipts from an active business of $300,000, deductions attributable to the active business of $100,000, dividend income of $120,000, capital gains on the sale of publicly traded stocks of $60,000, and expenses to earn the

dividend income of $30,000. What are the tax consequences to Y Corp. and to A?

C. BUILT-IN GAIN TAX

1. Macadam Corp. was formed seven years ago and did not elect S corporation status until January 1 of this year. It conducts a parking lot business near Enormous State University. Adam is its sole shareholder. Macadam Corp. has neither Subchapter C accumulated earnings and profits nor any NOLs. As of January 1, 2006, Macadam Corp. had the following assets:

Asset	Adjusted Basis	F.M.V.
Blackacre	$60,000	$40,000
Whiteacre	$20,000	$50,000
Greenacre	$35,000	$65,000

All three parcels of land are nondepreciable gravel parking lots. What are the shareholder and corporate level tax consequences of the following alternative transactions?

(a) (1) This year, Macadam Corp. sold Whiteacre for $65,000; its taxable income for this year if it were not an S corporation would have been $100,000.

(2) This year, Macadam Corp. sold Whiteacre for $60,000; its taxable income for this year if it were not an S corporation would have been $15,000.

(b) This year, Macadam Corp. sold Blackacre for $30,000 and sold Greenacre for $60,000; its taxable income for this year if it were not an S corporation would have been $90,000.

(c) This year, Macadam Corp. sold Blackacre for $50,000 and sold Greenacre for $70,000; its taxable income for this year if it were not an S corporation would have been $90,000.

(d) (1) This year, Macadam Corp. sold Whiteacre for $60,000 and sold Greenacre for $70,000; its taxable income for this year if it were not an S corporation would have been $90,000.

(2) This year, Macadam Corp. sold Whiteacre for $60,000 and sold Greenacre for $70,000; its taxable income for this year if it were not an S corporation would have been $90,000. Macadam Corp. had an unused NOL carryover from a prior C corporation year of $15,000.

(e) Six years from now, Macadam Corp. sells Whiteacre for $95,000.

PART IV

AFFILIATED CORPORATIONS

CHAPTER 18

AFFILIATED CORPORATIONS

SECTION 1. TAX REDUCTION WITH MULTIPLE CORPORATE TAXPAYERS

B. SECTIONS 1561 AND 1563

1. (a) X Corporation owns 800 shares of the voting common stock of Y Corporation, which is worth $800,000. Y Corporation also has outstanding 250 shares of voting participating preferred stock, worth $300,000, which is owned by the Independent Buggy Whip Craftsman's Association Pension Fund. Y Corporation owns 80 percent of the voting common stock of Z Corporation. There are no other classes of Z Corporation stock outstanding. The remainder of the Z Corporation stock is owned by Wooden Racing Scullmaker's Guild Pension Fund. The taxable income of each of the corporations is as follows:

Corporation	Taxable Income
X	$50,000
Y	$25,000
Z	$75,000

What is the income tax liability of each of X Corporation, Y Corporation and Z Corporation?

(b) Would your answer change if Y Corporation's voting common stock had two votes per share and the voting participating preferred stock owned by the Independent Buggy Whip Craftsman's Association Pension Fund had only one vote per share, but their values were not changed.

2. The stock of X Corporation, Y Corporation and Z Corporation is owned by unrelated individuals A, B, C, and D as follows.

Shareholder	X Corporation	Y Corporation	Z Corporation
A	73%	79%	29%
B	25%	1%	40%
C	1%	10%	20%
D	1%	10%	11%

Which of X Corporation, Y Corporation and Z Corporation are component members of a controlled group limited to a single use of the graduated rates in § 11?

SECTION 2. CONSOLIDATED RETURNS

1. T Corp. has two classes of stock outstanding. Class A is voting common stock and Class B is preferred stock. The management of P Corp. is considering the acquisition of some, but not all, of the outstanding stock of T Corp.

(a) Will P Corp. and T Corp. be eligible to file consolidated returns in the following alternative situations?

(1) The class B preferred is limited as to dividends and liquidation rights and is nonvoting except as required by state law. Each class of stock has 100 shares outstanding. P Corp. acquires 80 percent of the common stock and 10 percent of the preferred stock.

(2) The class B preferred stock is limited as to dividends and liquidation rights but is entitled to vote on a par with the Class A voting stock. Each class has 100 shares outstanding. P Corp.

acquires 90 percent of the common stock and 75 percent of the preferred stock.

(i) Assume the Class A stock is worth $50 per share and the class B stock is worth $100 per share.

(ii) Assume the Class A stock is worth $49 per share and the class B stock is worth $100 per share.

(3) The class B preferred stock is nonvoting, but after satisfaction of its preference participates with common as to dividends and liquidation rights. There are 800 shares of class A common outstanding and 200 shares of class B shares outstanding. P Corp. acquires 79 percent of the common stock and 100 percent of the preferred stock.

(4) The class A stock is voting common stock. There are 9,000 shares of class A stock, worth $9,000,000. The class B stock is voting participating preferred stock. There are 1,000 shares of class B stock, worth $1,000,000. The voting rights of the Class A and Class B stock are identical, one vote per share, except that the board of directors is classified. The class A stock collectively and solely elects seven directors, and the class B stock collectively and solely elects three directors. P Corp. acquires all of the Class A stock and none of the class B stock.

(b) Why should the P Corp. management be concerned about the ability to file consolidated returns?

2. (a) P Corporation owns 80 percent of X Corp., and X Corp. owns 80 percent of Y Corp. May all three corporations join in a consolidated return?

(b) P Corporation owns 100 percent of Maple Leaf, Inc. a Canadian corporation, and Maple Leaf owns 100 percent of Glacier, Inc., a Montana corporation, which in turn owns 90 percent of Black Hill Corp., a South Dakota corporation. Which of the corporations are eligible to join in a consolidated return?

(c) P Corp. owns 80 percent of X Corp. and Y Corp. X Corp. and Y Corp. each own 50 percent of Z Corp. May Z Corp. be included in a consolidated return with the other corporations?

3. On January 1, 2004, Empire Holding Corp., a publicly held corporation, purchased all of the outstanding stock of the Bluegrass Bourbon Distillery, Inc. for $3,000,000. For all relevant years Empire Holding Corp. and Bluegrass Bourbon Distillery filed consolidated returns.

(a) For the years 2004 through 2014, Bluegrass Bourbon Distillery had an aggregate operating loss of $4,000,000. On January 1, 2015, Empire Holding Corp. sold all of the outstanding stock of Bluegrass Bourbon Distillery to Kentucky Industrial Hemp Corp. for $100,000. How much gain or loss does Empire recognize?

(b) For the years 2004 through 2014, Bluegrass Bourbon Distillery had an aggregate operating loss of $4,000,000. The Distillery ceased operations on January 1, 2015, and all of its assets, which you may assume for simplicity had a zero basis, were abandoned as worthless. How much gain or loss does Empire recognize?

4. Several years ago P Corp. formed S Corp. by contributing assets of an operating division with a combined basis of $1,000,000, subject to liabilities of $3,000,000, which S Corp. assumed, in exchange for 10 shares of stock. P and S filed consolidated returns. Over the period S has been a member of the consolidated group, its income has exactly equaled its losses. This year, P Corp. sold 5 shares of S Corp. to X Corp. for $10,000,000. What are the tax consequences to P Corp. from the sale of the 5 shares of S Corp. stock?

5. X Corp. owns all of the stock of Y Corp., which in turn owns all of the stock of Z Corp. X Corp., Y Corp., and Z Corp. file consolidated returns. None of the corporations have any accumulated earnings and profits. This year X Corp. had $100,000 of earnings and profits, Y Corp. lost $400,000 (as measured for earnings and profits), and Z Corp. had earnings and profits of $1,000,000.

   (a) If X Corp. distributes $300,000 to its shareholders this year, what portion of the $300,000 is a dividend?

   (b) If none of the corporations has any profit or loss next year and X Corporation distributes $200,000 to its shareholders, what portion of the $200,000 is a dividend?

   (c) None of the corporations have any accumulated earnings and profits before last year. Last year X Corp. had $100,000 of earnings and profits, Y Corp. lost $400,000 (as measured for earnings and profits), and Z Corp. had earnings and profits of $1,000,000. On the first day of this year, X Corp, sold Y Corp. and realized neither gain nor loss. Later this year, Z Corp. distributed $300,000 to its new shareholders, even though Z Corp. had no current earnings and profits. What portion of the $300,000 is a dividend?

6. Petro, Inc. owns all of the stock of Leviathan Energy Corp. and Georges Bank Oil Drilling Corp. The three corporations file a consolidated

return. In 2006, Leviathan sold a mineral lease to Georges Bank for $5,000,000. Leviathan had a basis in the lease of $1,000,000.

(a) What are the tax consequences to Leviathan and Georges Bank if in 2007, Georges Bank sells the lease to an unrelated party for $6,000,000?

(b) What are the tax consequences to Leviathan and Georges Bank if in 2007, Georges Bank sells the lease to an unrelated party for $3,000,000?

(c) What are the tax consequences to Leviathan if in 2007 Georges Bank extracts oil from the purchased deposit, and on the basis that 10 percent of the deposit was extracted, Georges Bank claims a cost depletion allowance under § 611 (analogous to depreciation) of $500,000, i.e., 10% of its cost basis for the oil lease?

(d) What are the tax consequences to Leviathan and Petro if in 2007 Petro sells all of the stock of Georges Bank to an unrelated party for an amount equal to its adjusted basis in the Georges Bank stock?

7. (a) P Corp. owns all of the stock of S Corp. Both corporations have over $1,000,000 of earnings and profits. Last year, S distributed an asset with a basis of $60,000 and fair market value of $100,000 to P. This year, P sold the asset to an unrelated party for $120,000. What are the tax consequences to S and to P?

   (a) (1) How does the answer change if S's basis in the asset was $160,000?

   (2) How does the answer change if S's basis in the asset was $160,000 and when the asset was worth $120,000, P distributed the asset to a P shareholder as a dividend distribution?

8. P Corp. owns all of the stock of X Corp. and Y Corp. X Corp owned 60 percent of the voting common stock of Z Corp. Its basis for the stock was $350. Y Corp. owned 40 percent of the voting common stock of Z Corp. Its basis for the stock was $250. Z Corp. liquidated and distributed Blackacre, with a basis of $ 200 and a fair market value of $600 to X Corp and distributed Whiteacre with a basis of $100 and a fair market value of $400 to Z Corp. What are the tax consequences?

9. Recall that in Problem 3 Empire Holding Corp. purchased all of the outstanding stock of the Bluegrass Bourbon Distillery, Inc. for $3,000,000 in 2004. For the years 2004 through 2014, Bluegrass Bourbon Distillery broke-even from operations. In December, 2014, Bluegrass Bourbon Distillery realized a gain of $2,000,000 on the sale

of a nondepreciable asset that it had purchased in 2001 for $100,000, and which was worth $1,000,000 on January 1, 1996. On January 1, 2015, Empire sold all of the outstanding stock of Bluegrass Bourbon Distillery to Kentucky Industrial Hemp Corp. for $3,500,000. At that time the aggregate basis of Bluegrass Bourbon Distillery's assets was 4,000,000 How much gain or loss does Empire recognize?

PART V

Corporate Acquisition Techniques

CHAPTER 19

Taxable Acquisitions: The Purchase and Sale of a Corporate Business

1. Seamus owns all of the stock of QBox, Inc. His basis for the stock is $1,000,000. QBox, Inc. has only one asset, a patent on a video game device and the integrated software. The patent has a basis of $3,000,000. Redmond Corp. desires to acquire the QBox patent.

   (a) What are the tax consequences for QBox, Seamus, and Redmond, if Redmond pays QBox $23,000,000 for the patent and QBox uses the net proceeds of the sale to enter the pharmaceutical business (changing its name to Plan Q Pill Company)?

(b) What are the tax consequences for QBox, Seamus, and Redmond, if Redmond pays QBox $23,000,000 for the patent and QBox liquidates?

(1) What are the tax consequences for QBox, Seamus, and Redmond, if Redmond pays Seamus $23,000,000 for all of the stock of QBox?

(2) What are the tax consequences for QBox, Seamus, and Redmond, if Redmond pays Seamus $16,000,000 for all of the stock of QBox?

(3) Why is it unlikely that Redmond would be willing to pay the same price for stock of QBox as it would be willing to pay for the assets of QBox and why is it likely that Seamus will be willing to accept less?

SECTION 1. ASSET SALES AND ACQUISITIONS

1. Great Midwest Corp. (GMC) produces alcohol from corn for use in the production of gasohol. It has 1000 shares of common stock outstanding, which are owned equally by Chip and Dale, its founders. Each of them has a basis in the stock of $1,000,000. It has two divisions, the Corn Products Division and the Gasohol Alcohol Products Division. Beyond Petrochemicals, Inc. (BP) has offered to purchase the Gasohol Alcohol Products Division and to employ the employees of the division to continue the business. The assets on the balance sheet (and estimates of the current fair market value of each asset) of GMC's Gasohol Alcohol Division are as follows:

Asset	F.M.V.	Basis
Marketable securities	$ 2,000,000	$ 1,000,000
Accounts receivable	$ 4,000,000	$ 5,000,000
Inventory	$ 7,000,000	$ 3,000,000
Land	$20,000,000	$10,000,000
Buildings & Improvements	$10,000,000	$ 7,000,000
Equipment	$ 2,000,000	$ 0
Patents	$ 5,000,000	$ 1,000,000

(a)(1) What are the tax consequences to all parties if BP pays GMC $65,000,000 for the Gasohol Alcohol Division?

(2) What are the tax consequences if BP also paid Chip and Dale $5,000,000 each in consideration of their personal agreement not to enter into the production of gasohol (or to acquire or hold a significant interest in another corporation engaged in the production of gasohol) any time in the next five years?

(3) How would your answer to part (a)(1) differ if GMC did not operate its two businesses directly, but instead operated the businesses through wholly owned limited liability companies, Corn Production, LLC. and Gasohol Alcohol Products, LLC., BP originally funded Gasohol Alcohol Products, LLC with $10,000,000 of cash to cover its start-up, and the sale was effected by GMC selling the sole membership unit in the LLC to BP for $65,000,000?

(4) How would your answer to part (a)(1) differ if GMC did not operate its two businesses directly, but instead operated the businesses through wholly owned subsidiaries, Corn Production Corp. and Gasohol Alcohol Products, Inc., and BP purchased the stock of Gasohol Alcohol Products, Inc., in which GMC had a $10,000,000 basis?

(b)(1) How would your answer to part (a)(1) differ if in addition to paying the $65,000,000 in cash, BP assumed a mortgage lien debt of $5,000,000 on the Gasohol Alcohol land and building?

(2) How would your answer to part (a)(1) differ if in addition to paying the $65,000,000 in cash, BP assumed $5,000,000 of accounts payable owed by the Gasohol Alcohol division?

(3) How would your answer to part (a)(1) differ if in addition to paying the $65,000,000 in cash, BP assumed any liability resulting from a pending products liability suit against GMC relating to the Gasohol Alcohol division? The suit sought $10,000,000 in damages, GMC and BP expected that there was only a 10 percent chance of losing the suit, and three years later a final judgment was entered awarding $9,000,000 to the plaintiff?

2. Cleo owned all of the stock of Lucretia Boat Corp., the sole asset of which was a cruise ship. The corporation's basis in the cruise ship was $5,000,000 and it had a fair market value of $25,000,000. The cruise ship was encumbered by a purchase money lien of $8,000,000. Cleo's basis in the stock was $3,000,000. Lucretia Boat Corp. sold the ship to Tully for $17,000,000 cash and Tully assumed the $8,000,000 debt. After paying the taxes due on the sale of its assets, Lucretia Boat Corp. liquidated and distributed all of its remaining cash to Cleo. What are the tax consequences?

3. Blips Broadcasting Corporation, the operator of radio station KPMG, a radio station famous for its 24/7 broadcasting of "tax savings tips for everyone," was acquired by Cono Corporation in a merger under the statutory provisions of the corporation laws of the states in which the two corporations were organized. Pursuant to the terms of the merger, Arthur, the sole shareholder of Blips Broadcasting, received 20-year

Cono bonds in the amount of $21,250,000 in exchange for his stock. Arthur had a basis of $6,250,000 in the stock. Blips Broadcasting Corporation's basis in the radio station KPMG assets was $5,000,000. What are the tax consequences to the parties (assuming that the corporate tax rate is a flat 35 %)?

4. Earle and Herman were equal shareholders of E&H Engineering Consultants, Inc., a cash method taxpayer engaged in the petroleum and civil engineering consulting businesses. Earle and Herman each have a basis of $100,000 in their stock. Beck Corporation, another engineering consulting corporation purchased the assets of E&H Engineering Consultants, Inc. for $10,000,000 in cash. In addition, Beck assumed a $1,000,000 debt E&H Engineering Consultants owed to the First National Bank of Kellogg, which E&H Engineering Consultants incurred to purchase equipment and $500,000 of accounts payable for items such as rent, utilities, local real estate taxes, and accrued but unpaid employee compensation. What is total amount realized by E&H Engineering Consultants, Inc. on the sale of its assets? What is Beck's aggregate basis in the assets it acquired? May Beck deduct any portion of the purchase price?

SECTION 2. STOCK SALES AND ACQUISITIONS

1. George owned all of the stock of Arpix, Inc., which produces software for 3D computer animation for the film industry. George's basis in the stock was $1,000,000. George sold all of the stock to Steve for $10,000,000 in cash. At that time Arpix owed $1,000,000 to the Millennium National Bank. Arpix asset's consisted of a copyright with a basis of $500,000 and computer equipment with a basis of $50,000.

   (a) What is total amount realized by George?

   (b) What is Steve's basis in the Arpix stock?

   (c) How much gain or loss does Arpix recognize?

   (d) What is Arpix basis in its assets?

2. West Electric Corporation produces and sells cellular telephones. Mabel owned all of the stock of West Electric. Mabel's basis for the stock was $2,000,000. West's assets on the balance sheet (and estimates of the current fair market value of each asset) are as follows:

Asset	Basis	F.M.V.
Marketable securities	$ 500,000	$ 600,000
Accounts receivable	$1,000,000	$ 900,000
Inventory	$1,000,000	$6,000,000
Land	$1,000,000	$2,500,000
Factory	$1,500,000	$4,000,000
Franchise agreements with cellular service providers	$ 0	$1,000,000
Patents	$ 0	$5,000,000

West Electric owed $5,000,000 to the Monopolistic National Bank. Centel Corp. purchased all of Mabel's stock of West Electric for cash.

(a)(1) What are the tax consequences to all parties if the cash purchase price was $16,250,000 and Centel does not make a § 338 election?

(2) What are the tax consequences to all parties if the cash purchase price was $16,250,000 and Centel makes a § 338 election?

(3) What are the tax consequences to all parties if the cash purchase price was $8,450,000 and Centel makes a § 338 election?

3. (a) Great Wall Automotive Corp. began purchasing stock of Studebaker Car Corporation on the New York Stock exchange on January 2 of last year. By April 15 of last year, Great Wall had acquired 21 percent of the stock of Studebaker. Between April 16 of last year and January 2 of this year Great Wall acquired an additional 58 percent of Studebaker, for a total of 79 percent. On April 17 of this year Great Wall acquired the remaining 21 percent of Studebaker from a single institutional investor. May Great Wall make a § 338 election with respect to Studebaker?

(b) Suppose that during a single calendar year Great Wall Automotive Corp. purchased exactly 80 percent of the stock of Studebaker Car Corporation in stock exchange transactions for an aggregate purchase price of $17,000,000. Studebaker's basis in its assets was $5,000,000 and it had no outstanding debts. If Great Wall makes a § 338 election with respect to Studebaker, what is the resulting aggregate basis in Studebaker's assets?

4. Earleton Boatworks, Inc. manufactures and sells bass-fishing boats. All of the stock of Earleton Boatworks is owned by Richard's & Son's Pecan Farm & Real Estate Development Corp. Earleton Boatworks, Inc.'s assets on the balance sheet (and estimates of the current fair market value of each asset) are as follows:

Asset	Basis	F.M.V.
Marketable securities	$ 500,000	$ 600,000
Accounts receivable	$1,000,000	$ 900,000
Inventory	$5,000,000	$6,000,000
Land	$1,000,000	$2,500,000
Factory	$1,500,000	$4,000,000
Franchise agreements with boat dealers	$ 0	$1,000,000
Patents	$ 0	$5,000,000
Goodwill	$ 0	$5,000,000

Earleton Boatworks owed $5,000,000 to the Gator National Bank. Earleton Boatworks and Richard's & Son's Pecan Farm & Real Estate Development Corp. file a consolidated return. If Bassamatic Corp. purchased all of the stock of Earleton Boatworks for $20,000,000 in cash, should Richard's & Son's and Bassamatic make a § 338(h)(10) election?

(a) Assume Richard's & Son's basis for its Earleton Boatworks stock was $3,000,000.

(b) Assume Richard's & Son's basis for its Earleton Boatworks stock was $7,000,000.

5. Enrico and Maria each own 50 of the 100 outstanding shares of common stock of Opticon Corporation, which has a valid Subchapter S election in effect. Enrico's basis in the Opticon stock is $6,000,000; Maria's basis in the Opticon stock is $4,000,000. Opticon manufactures opera glasses. The assets recorded on its balance sheet consist of the following:

Asset	Basis	FMV
Inventory	$ 1,000,000	$ 9,000,000
Factory Land	$ 5,000,000	$ 6,000,000
Factory Building	$ 5,000,000	$ 5,000,000
Equipment	$ 3,000,000	$ 2,000,000
Patent	$ 4,000,000	$ 8,000,000
TOTAL	$18,000,000	$30,000,000

Opticon has one liability; it owes the Last National Bank $5,000,000. Hubble Opticals, Inc. has proposed to purchase all of the Opticon stock either (1) for $26,000,000 in cash ($13,000,000 each) if Enrico and Maria agree to make a §338(h)(10) election, or (2) $24,000,000 in cash ($12,000,000 each) if there is no §338(h)(10) election. Enrico and Maria want to sell. Which offer should they accept? Why?

6. Assume that individual A owns all of the stock of P Corp., which in turn owns all of the stock of T Corp. A's basis for the stock of P is $100, and the fair market value of the stock is $500. P Corp.'s only asset is the T Corp. stock, with a basis of $100 and a fair market value of $500. T Corp. has assets with a basis of $100 and a fair market value of $500. (Note that T Corp.'s assets are the only tangible property involved in the problem.)

   (a) If P liquidates T and sells the T assets to individual B for $500, after which P liquidates and distributes the cash to A, what are the tax consequences?

   (b) If P sells the stock of T to B for $500, after which B liquidates T and A liquidates P, what are the tax consequences?

   (c) How do you explain any difference in your answers to questions (a) and (b) in light of the fact that the end results are the same?

7. T Corporation, a publicly traded corporation, has a fair market value of $40 - $60 million. Y Corp. proposes either (a) to purchase all of the T common stock for $60 million of convertible notes payable in 15 years at 10% interest or (b) to exchange a 10% preferred stock of $50 million for all the X Corp. common stock. Are the proposals of equivalent costs and value? Do any of the following provisions apply:

   (a) § 279,
   (b) § 163(e),
   (c) § 385, or
   (d) § 163(j)?

CHAPTER 20

DISTRIBUTIONS MADE IN CONNECTION WITH THE SALE OF A CORPORATE BUSINESS: "BOOTSTRAP" ACQUISITIONS

SECTION 1. BOOTSTRAP TRANSACTIONS INVOLVING INDIVIDUALS: CAPITAL GAIN VERSUS ORDINARY INCOME

1. Al, Georgiana, and Pete each owned one third of the outstanding common stock of the Pocatello Raiders Football Club, Inc. The three shareholders signed a contract under which on the death of any shareholder the remaining shareholders would purchase the stock of the deceased shareholder from his or her estate at a price set by a formula in the contract. The Pocatello Raiders insured the lives of all three shareholders with Pari-Mutuel Insurance Co. This year Al died and Pocatello Raiders received life insurance proceeds that it used to redeem Al's stock.

   (a) What are the tax consequences?

   (b) If the shareholders had come to you for advice last year, how would you have suggested that they amend their contract?

2. A owned 40 shares of stock of X Corp. common stock and B owned the other 60 shares. Consider the following alternative transactions.

   (a) Pursuant to a prearranged plan, X Corp. redeemed 5 shares from A on April 15th, and on July 1st, A sold 10 shares to C. Does A's redemption on April 15th qualify under § 302(a)?

   (b) Pursuant to a prearranged plan, X Corp. redeemed 18 shares from B on April 15th, and on July 1st, B sold 1 share to A. Does B's redemption on April 15th qualify under § 302(a)?

3. Hillary and William own as joint tenants all of the stock of Management Of New & Incumbent Candidates Advocacy, Inc., which is engaged in

the business of managing political and initiative campaigns. The shares of the corporation are Hillary's and William's principal asset. Hillary's and William's combined basis in the stock is $80,000. The fair market value of the stock is $200,000. Hillary and William have filed for divorce (irreconcilable political differences). Hillary will continue to own the corporation. William will be paid for his interest in cash. The only cash available is in the corporation, which also can borrow to pay off William. Hillary and William agree in the divorce settlement that one-half of the corporate shares will be deemed to belong to William and that Hillary will cause the corporation to redeem William's shares for cash. What are the tax consequences of the redemption distribution to Hillary and William?

SECTION 2. BOOTSTRAP TRANSACTIONS INVOLVING CORPORATIONS

1. (a) Cumberland Consolidated Corporation (CCC) is the sole shareholder of Natural Bridge Mining Corp. CCC and Natural Bridge do not file a consolidated return, and CCC has held its Natural Bridge stock for more than two years. CCC has a $150,000 basis in its Natural Bridge stock. Lake Island Coal Corporation is a prospective buyer and is willing to purchase all of the Natural Bridge stock, but it is unable to pay the $500,000 price demanded by CCC even though it believes the price is fair. Natural Bridge has $100,000 of cash on hand and $170,000 of accumulated earnings and profits. To solve these problems, the parties have agreed on the following plan. CCC will cause Natural Bridge to distribute $100,000 to it as a dividend. Promptly thereafter, CCC will sell its Natural Bridge stock to Lake Island Coal Corp. for $400,000. What are the tax consequences of this plan?

   (b) Assume that CCC held only 75% of the stock of Natural Bridge and that the remaining 25% was held by Gregory Macomber (an individual). What would Macomber think of this plan? How might he want to change the plan? Does Macomber's basis for his stock affect how he views the plan?

CHAPTER 21

TAX FREE ACQUISITIVE REORGANIZATIONS

SECTION 2. THE FUNDAMENTAL RULES GOVERNING REORGANIZATIONS

A. THE BASIC STATUTORY SCHEME

1. Which of the following transactions are eligible to qualify as a reorganization as defined in § 368. If the transaction qualifies, which subsection of § 368 applies?

   (a)(1) Pursuant to a state law statute governing mergers, T Corp. is merged into P Corp. The T Corp. shareholders surrender their stock, which is cancelled, in exchange for P Corp. voting common stock.

   (2) Pursuant to state law statute governing mergers, T Corp. is merged into P Corp. The T Corp. shareholders surrender their stock, which is cancelled, in exchange for P Corp. nonvoting preferred stock.

   (3) Pursuant to state law statute governing mergers, T Corp. is merged into P Corp. The T Corp. shareholders surrender their stock, which is cancelled, in exchange for P Corp. 25-year sinking fund 6% debentures.

   (4) Pursuant to state law statute governing mergers, T Corp. is merged into P Corp. The T Corp. shareholders surrender their stock, which is cancelled, in exchange for P Corp. voting common stock. Immediately after the merger of T Corp. into P. Corp., P Corp. transfers all of the T Corp. assets to its newly formed wholly owned subsidiary, S Corp.

   (5) Pursuant to state law statute governing mergers, T Corp. is merged into PS LLC, a limited liability company wholly owned by P Corp. The T Corp. shareholders surrender their stock, which is cancelled, in exchange for P Corp. voting common stock.

(b)(1) P Corp. makes a tender offer directly to the shareholders of T Corp. to acquire the T Corp. stock in an exchange of one share of P Corp. voting common stock for each share of T Corp. stock.

(i) Eighty percent of the shareholders of T Corp. accept the tender offer.

(ii) Seventy-nine percent of T Corp. shareholders accept the tender offer.

(2) P Corp. makes a tender offer to the shareholders of T Corp. to acquire the T Corp. stock in an exchange of one share of P Corp. nonvoting common stock for each share of T Corp. stock, and all of the shareholders of T Corp. accept the offer.

(3) P Corp. makes a tender offer to the shareholders of T Corp. to acquire the T Corp. stock in an exchange of one share of P Corp. voting common stock, worth $95 and $5 of cash, for each share of T Corp. stock, and all of the shareholders of T Corp. accept the offer.

(4) S Corp., a wholly owned subsidiary of P Corp. makes a tender offer to the shareholders of T Corp. of one share of P Corp. voting preferred stock for each share of T Corp. stock. Eighty percent of the shareholders of T Corp. accept the tender offer.

(5) P Corp. makes a tender offer to the shareholders of T Corp. to acquire the T Corp. stock in an exchange of one share of P Corp. voting common stock for each share of T Corp. stock, and all of the shareholders of T Corp. accept the offer. Immediately after the acquisition of the T Corp. stock, P Corp. transfers all of the T Corp. stock to its newly formed wholly owned subsidiary, S Corp.

(c)(1)(i) Pursuant to a purchase and sale agreement, T Corp. transfers all of its assets to P Corp., which assumes all of T Corp.'s liabilities ($200,000), for 1000 shares of voting common stock of P Corp., worth $1,000,000. T Corp. liquidates and distributes the stock to its shareholders.

(ii) What if T Corp. does not liquidate?

(2) Pursuant to a purchase and sale agreement, T Corp. transfers all of its assets to P Corp., which assumes all of X Corp.'s liabilities ($200,000), for 900 shares of voting common stock of P Corp., worth $ 900,000 and $100,000 of cash. T Corp. liquidates and distributes the stock to its shareholders.

(3) Pursuant to a purchase and sale agreement, T Corp. transfers all of its assets to S Corp., 80 percent of the stock of which is owned by P Corp., for 1000 shares of voting preferred stock of P Corp., worth $1,000,000. T Corp. liquidates and distributes the P Corp. stock to its shareholders.

(4) Pursuant to a purchase and sale agreement, T Corp. transfers all of its assets to P Corp. in exchange for 1000 shares of voting common stock of P Corp. T Corp. liquidates and distributes the stock to its shareholders. Immediately after the merger of T Corp. into P. Corp., P Corp. transfers all of the T Corp. assets to its newly formed wholly owned subsidiary, S Corp.

(d) Pursuant to state law statute governing mergers, T Corp. is merged into S Corp., a wholly owned subsidiary of P Corp.

(1) The T Corp. shareholders surrender their stock, which is cancelled, for P Corp. voting common stock.

(2) The T Corp. shareholders surrender their stock, which is cancelled, for P Corp. nonvoting common stock.

(e) Pursuant to state law statute governing mergers, S Corp., a wholly owned subsidiary of P Corp. is merged into T Corp.

(1) The T Corp. shareholders surrender their stock, which is cancelled, in exchange for P Corp. voting stock. P Corp. exchanges its S Corp. stock, which is cancelled, for newly issued T Corp. stock, which then constitutes 100 % of the T Corp. outstanding stock.

(2) The T Corp. shareholders surrender their stock, which is cancelled, for P Corp. nonvoting preferred stock. P Corp. exchanges its S Corp. stock, which is cancelled, for newly issued T Corp. stock, which then constitutes 100 % of the T Corp. outstanding stock.

(f) (1) T Corp., which is equally owned by A, B, and C, sold all of its assets to P Corp., the voting common stock of which was equally owned by C and D, for 600 shares of P Corp nonvoting preferred stock. T Corp. liquidated and distributed the P Corp nonvoting preferred stock equally among A, B, and C.

(2) T Corp., which is equally owned by A and B sold all of its assets to P Corp., in which B, C and D each originally owned 100 shares of voting common stock, for 150 shares of P Corp voting common stock. T Corp. liquidated and distributed the P Corp stock equally between A and B.

2. P Corp. owned 80 percent of the voting common stock of S Corp. Fiona owned the other 20 percent of the voting common stock of S Corp. Pursuant to state law governing mergers, S Corp. merged into P Corp. The S Corp. stock owned by P Corp. was cancelled, and Fiona received P. Corp. nonvoting preferred stock. How is the transaction characterized for each of P Corp., S Corp., and Fiona?

3. Pursuant to state law governing mergers, T Corp. merged into P Corp. The T Corp. shareholders surrendered their stock, which was cancelled, in exchange for P Corp. voting common stock. Immediately after the merger of T Corp. into P. Corp., P Corp. transferred 40 percent of the T Corp. assets to X Corp. a wholly owned subsidiary of P Corp.'s wholly owned subsidiary, S1 Corp., and P Corp. transferred 60 percent of the T Corp. assets to Y Corp., a wholly owned subsidiary of P Corp.'s wholly owned subsidiary, S2 Corp. Does the merger of T Corp. into P Corp. qualify under § 368(a)(1)(A)?

4. T Corp., which is publicly held, merged into P Corp., which also is publicly held, in a transaction that qualified under § 368(a)(1)(A). Nadine owned 1,000 shares of T Corp. stock that was surrendered in the merger. How much gain must Nadine recognize under the following circumstances? What is Nadine's basis in any P Corp. stock received?

   (a) Nadine's basis for the T Corp. stock was $10,000 and Nadine received 1,000 shares of P Corp. stock worth $100,000.

   (b) Nadine's basis for the T Corp. stock was $10,000 and Nadine received 800 shares of P Corp. stock worth $80,000 and $20,000 cash.

   (c) Nadine's basis for the T Corp. stock was $85,000 and Nadine received 800 shares of P Corp. stock worth $80,000 and $20,000 cash.

   (d) Nadine's basis for the T Corp. stock was $130,000 and Nadine received 800 shares of P Corp. stock worth $80,000 and $20,000 cash.

   (e) Nadine's basis for the T Corp. stock was $10,000 and Nadine received 800 shares of P Corp. stock worth $80,000 and a P Corp. debt instrument due in thirty years, with a principal amount of $20,000.

B. THE CONTINUITY OF INTEREST REQUIREMENT

(1) QUALITATIVE AND QUANTITATIVE ASPECTS

1. P Corporation acquires T pursuant to a state law statutory merger. Assume that apart from the continuity of interest requirement, all other requirements for a tax free reorganization under § 368(a)(1)(A),

are satisfied. Given the following *alternative* additional facts, consider whether or not a tax free reorganization has occurred.

(a) P acquires T solely for P's voting common stock and the former T shareholders become shareholders of P. After the merger, each of the five former shareholders of T own approximately 1% in value of the outstanding common stock of Y.

(b) Would your answer change if the former T shareholders received nonvoting common stock of P?

(c) Would your answer change if the former T shareholders received P Corp. nonvoting preferred stock with a par value and fair market value of $20,000,000?

(d) Would your answer change if instead of issuing stock, P acquired T by issuing to the former T shareholders 11% bonds due in the year 2075 with an aggregate face value of $10,000,000 which are securities for purposes of § 354?

2. T Corporation is owned equally by Franklin, Gert, Harvey, Irene, and Jose. P Corporation acquires T pursuant to a statutory merger. Assume that all requirements for a tax free reorganization under I.R.C. § 368(a)(1)(A), apart from continuity of interest, are satisfied. Given the following *alternative* additional facts, consider whether or not a tax free reorganization has occurred.

   (a) P Corp. acquires T Corp. for 100,000 shares of P Corp. voting common stock, worth $10,000,000 and $10,000,000 cash. Franklin, Gert, Harvey, Irene, and Jose each receive 20,000 shares of P Corp. stock (F.M.V., $2,000,000) and $2,000,000 cash.

   (b) Would your answer differ if P Corp. acquires T Corp. for 80,000 shares of P Corp. voting common stock, worth $8,000,000 and $12,000,000 cash? Franklin, Gert, Harvey, Irene, and Jose each receive 16,000 shares of P Corp. stock (F.M.V., $1,600,000) and $2,400,000 cash.

   (c) Would your answer differ if P Corp. acquires T Corp. for 60,000 shares of P Corp. voting common stock, worth $6,000,000 and $14,000,000 cash? Franklin, Gert, Harvey, Irene, and Jose each receive 12,000 shares of P Corp. stock (F.M.V., $1,200,000) and $2,800,000 cash.

   (d) Would your answer differ if Franklin, Gert, Harvey, Irene, and Jose received the following consideration ($ are in $1,000's):

Shareholder	Cash	P Shares (F.M.V.)
Franklin	$ 6,000	$ 0
Gert	$ 6,000	$ 0
Harvey	$ 3,500	$ 500
Irene	$ 500	$3,500
Jose	$ 0	$4,000
	$12,000	$8,000

Is this a reorganization? Which shareholders are affected by whether it is a reorganization? Which shareholders are not affected by whether it is a reorganization?

3. P Corporation acquires T pursuant to a state law statutory merger. The consideration issued to the T shareholders by P consists of (1) $2,500,000 worth of P Corp. voting common stock, (2) bonds, which are securities for purposes of § 354, with a $4,000,000 principal amount, and (3) $3,500,000 cash. Has a tax free reorganization occurred?

4. P Corp and T Corp are publicly traded. P Corp and T Corp entered into a merger agreement that provided for the merger of T into P. The agreed upon exchange was that each share of T would be surrendered in exchange for one share of P common stock and $55 cash. The merger agreement had no provision to adjust the exchange ratio to reflect stock price fluctuations between the date of the merger agreement and the effective date of the merger (the closing). On the day before the merger agreement, P stock was trading at $45 per share. On the date of the merger (the closing), P stock was trading at $25 per share. Has a tax free reorganization occurred?

5. P Corp and T Corp are publicly traded. P Corp and T Corp entered into a merger agreement that provided for the merger of T into P. The merger agreement provided that each share of T would be surrendered in exchange for (1) two shares of P common stock, and (2) at the election of each T shareholder, either two additional shares of P Common stock or $80 cash. The merger agreement had no provision to adjust the exchange ratio to reflect stock price fluctuations between the date of the merger agreement and the effective date of the merger (the closing). On the day before the merger agreement, P stock was trading at $40 per share. On the date of the merger (the closing), P stock was trading at $20 per share. All of the former T shareholders elected to receive only $80 of cash. Has a tax free reorganization occurred?

6. Andrea, Barry, and Chantal own all of the common stock of T Corporation. Dean, Erin, and Felix collectively own T Corporation bonds due in 2075 in the principal amount of $5,000,000. The fair

market value of all of the T Corporation assets is $3,000,000. Pursuant to a purchase and sale agreement, T Corporation transferred all of its assets to P Corp. in exchange for 3,000 shares of 6%, $1,000 par value voting preferred stock. T Corporation dissolved and distributed the 3,000 shares of the P Corp. preferred stock to Dean, Erin, and Felix. In the dissolution of T Corp., Andrea, Barry, and Chantal received nothing in exchange for their T Corp. stock, which was cancelled. Has a tax free reorganization has occurred?

(2) TEMPORAL ASPECTS

1. Gordon and Helene each owned 50 percent of the outstanding stock of T Corporation. P Corporation, which is not publicly traded, offered to acquire T Corporation in a statutory merger in which 100 percent of the consideration would be P Corporation voting common stock. Gordon and Helene wanted cash rather than P Corporation stock, but P Corporation refused to pay cash. Thereupon, Gordon and Helene sold their T Corporation stock for cash to Isaac, who was unrelated to Gordon, Helene or P Corporation, but whose participation in the transaction was suggested by P Corporation. Following the sale, Isaac, acting on behalf of T Corporation, accepted the Y Corporation proposal and voted to merge T Corporation into P Corporation in a statutory merger in which 100 percent of the consideration was P Corporation stock. Does the merger qualify as a tax-free reorganization? Why does it matter?

2. (a) Jerry and Karen each owned 50 percent of the outstanding stock of T Corporation. P Corporation, which is not publicly traded, offered to acquire T Corporation in a statutory merger in which 100 percent of the consideration would be P Corporation voting common stock. Jerry and Karen wanted cash rather than stock in P Corporation, but P Corporation refused to pay cash. P Corporation informed Jerry and Karen that within a year P Corporation was going to make an initial public offering, and once the P Corporation stock was publicly traded, P Corporation would facilitate the sale of its stock received by Jerry and Karen in the merger through stock exchange transactions. After a contract to this effect was executed, Jerry and Karen thereupon voted to merge T Corporation into P Corporation. Jerry and Karen received P Corporation stock in the merger and seven months later, after P Corporation went public, Jerry and Karen sold in a New York Stock Exchange transaction all of the P Corporation stock received in the merger. Does the merger qualify as a tax-free reorganization?

   (b) Suppose that the contract between Jerry and Karen and P Corporation also provided that if P Corporation was not taken public within a year of the merger that P Corporation would secure a purchaser for the P Corporation stock received in the merger by Jerry and Karen. If P Corporation did not go public and P Corporation arranged a purchase of the P Corporation stock received by Jerry and Karen, does the merger qualify as a tax-free reorganization under the following circumstances:

(1) P Corporation redeemed the stock.

(2) P Corporation caused its wholly owned subsidiary, S Corporation, to purchase the stock.

(3) Lorenzo, the president of P Corporation, purchased the stock with Lorenzo's own funds.

(4) P Corporation arranged with Goldman-Lynch Investment Bankers that Goldman-Lynch would purchase the stock.

3. Melissa, Noel, and Olga each owned one-third of the outstanding common stock of T Corp. Melissa and Noel sold their stock (in the aggregate representing two-thirds of the outstanding stock) to P Corp. for cash. Olga refused to sell. Immediately after obtaining two-thirds voting control, P Corp. voted its shares in favor of merging T Corp. into S Corp., a wholly owned subsidiary of P Corp. Pursuant to the merger, Olga received voting common stock of P Corp. P Corp.'s stock in T Corp. was cancelled.

   (a) Is the merger a tax-free statutory merger under § 368(a)(2)(D)? If not, what is it?

   (b) Assume alternatively that Melissa and Noel each owned forty percent of the stock of T Corp. and received all cash for their shares. In the subsequent merger Olga received P Corp. stock for her twenty percent of the T Stock. Is this transaction a tax-free merger? How will the two corporations treat the transaction? How will Olga treat the transaction?

4. Pablo, Rebekah, and Sebastian each owned one-third of the outstanding common stock of T Corp. P Corp., which is not publicly traded, offered to acquire T Corp. in a statutory merger in which 100 percent of the consideration would be P Corp. voting common stock. Pablo was willing to accept the offer, but Rebekah and Sebastian wanted cash rather than stock in P Corp. and P Corp. refused to pay cash. To effectuate the merger, with P Corp.'s consent, T Corp. sold obsolete assets that were no longer useful in its business for cash and used the cash to redeem the Rebekah's and Sebastian's stock. Thereafter, T merged into P Corp., which thereby obtained T's modern business assets which it put to immediate use. In the merger, Pablo received P voting common

stock in exchange for his T stock, which was cancelled. Is the merger a tax-free statutory merger under § 368(a)(1)(A)?

C. CONTINUITY OF BUSINESS ENTERPRISE

1. P Corporation acquires T Corporation pursuant to a statutory merger. Assume that all statutory requirements for a tax free reorganization are satisfied, apart from the continuity of business enterprise requirement. Given the following alternative additional facts, consider whether or not a tax free reorganization has occurred:

   (a) P issues common stock for all of the assets of T. T's assets consist solely of stock and short-term securities. These assets were purchased with cash from a recent sale to an unrelated corporation of T's operating assets formerly used in its gizmo business. P Corp. is engaged in manufacturing widgets and it plans to sell the stock and short-term securities obtained from T Corp. to raise cash to construct a new widget factory.

   (b) Would your answer differ if P used T's cash to construct a new gizmo factory?

2. Assume that T Corp. did not sell its gizmo business prior to the merger and it was engaged in manufacturing gizmos. P was engaged in manufacturing widgets. T merged into P and P continued T's gizmo operation. Three weeks after the merger, P sold its widgets operation to an unrelated party.

3. Assume that up until three years prior to the merger, T historically engaged in manufacturing gizmos and that P engages in manufacturing widgets. Approximately three years prior to the merger T sold its assets for cash and invested in short-term securities. One year prior to the merger T invested substantially all its funds in an apartment project. Subsequent to the merger P continued to own and operate the apartment project and to manufacture widgets.

4. (a) Assume that T manufactured gizmos, gadgets and bassamatics. Immediately after the merger P sold T's gizmo and gadget businesses and used the cash to expand the bassamatic business.

   (b) What if P used the cash to expand its widget business?

   (c) What if P used the cash to expand its widget business, discontinued the bassamatic business, but converted the bassamatic assets to manufacturing widgets?

5. (a) P and T were competitors in the same product line. P acquired all of the assets of T in a statutory merger, and after the merger P retired all of T's assets except a customer list, which it used to sell products made using P's preexisting plant.

   (b) P and T were competitors in the same product line. P acquired all of the assets of T in a statutory merger, and after the merger P retired all of T's assets, but it held T's former factory in reserve (and maintained it) in case P's assets broke down.

6. T Corp. was engaged in manufacturing fishing equipment. P was engaged in manufacturing hunting equipment. P acquired T in a transaction in which T merged into P's wholly owned subsidiary, S, in a forward triangular merger described in § 368(a)(2)(D). The day after the merger, X Corp. made an offer to P to purchase all of the stock of S Corp. for cash, which included all of the T assets. P agreed to sell S Corp. and as expeditiously as possible the transaction closed.

7. (a) T Corp. was engaged in manufacturing gizmos. P was engaged in manufacturing widgets. T merged into P, and P promptly transferred T's gizmo operation to S Corporation, its wholly owned subsidiary.

   (b) T manufactured gizmos, gadgets, bassamatics, and whirligigs. T merged into P, and P transferred the gizmo business to W Corp., the gadget business to X Corp. the bassamatic business to Y Corp., and the Whirligig business to Z Corp. Z Corp, is an 80 percent controlled subsidiary of Y Corp., which is an 80 percent controlled subsidiary of X Corp., which is an 80 percent controlled subsidiary of W Corp., which is an 80 percent controlled subsidiary of S Corp., which is an 80 percent controlled subsidiary of P Corp.

8. P owns no assets other than the stock of R Corp. and S Corp., both of which manufacture and sell widgets. T owns no assets other than the stock of U Corp. and W Corp., both of which manufacture and sell gizmos. P acquires all of the assets of T in a statutory merger.

9. T and P are both controlled by Oscar, Patty, and Rafael. P was organized 20 years ago as a franchised wholesaler of widgets. T was formed three years ago to independently engage in the manufacture of widgets. T has never been successful and for the last six months its activities have been largely suspended. Manufacturing activities never reached beyond the preliminary stage. P acquires all of the assets of T in a statutory merger. Immediately prior to the merger T had net operating loss carry forwards of $150,000.

D. JUDICIAL LIMITATIONS

(1) BUSINESS PURPOSE

1. Calvin owned all of the stock of True Believer Publishers, Inc. Calvin's basis for the stock was $4,000,000. Gimmie Shelter, Inc., offered to acquire all of the stock of True Believer in exchange for 60,000 shares of Gimmie Shelter, worth $3,000,000 (trading at $50 per share on the NYSE). Calvin counter-offered for 59,000 shares, worth $2,950,000 and $25,000 in cash. Gimmie Shelter accepted the counter-offer and acquired all of the stock of True Believer for 59,000 shares of Gimmie Shelter, worth $2,950,000, and $25,000 in cash. Calvin claimed a $1,025,000 capital loss on his tax return. Calvin has been audited and the IRS asserts that there was no business purpose for the injection of cash into the deal and that Calvin's loss should be disallowed. Assess Calvin's chances of prevailing in litigation of the issue.

(2) STEP TRANSACTION DOCTRINE

1. Paul owned a large parcel of land with a basis of $100,000. In January BigBox Store Corp. asked Paul if he was interested in selling the land to BigBox for $10,000,000 in cash, or BigBox stock worth $10,000,000, or a combination of both. The offer was open until April 15. On February 1st, pursuant to advice from his C.P.A., Ernie Whinney, Paul transferred the land to newly formed Holding Corp. in a § 351 transfer. Paul owned all of the outstanding stock of Holding Corp. On March 1st, Paul counter-offered to BigBox's offer, stating that he would accept $10,000,000 of BigBox voting common stock (publicly traded on the NASDAQ system) in exchange for all of the stock of Holding Corp. This offer was accepted by BigBox and the deal was closed on April 1st. Shortly thereafter, Holding Corp. was dissolved and the land was distributed to BigBox in a § 332 liquidation. Ernie Whinney has advised Paul that the transaction with BigBox was a valid tax free reorganization. Is he correct?

2. Debby owned all of the stock of Cleveland Rock & Opera Recording Corp. Debby's basis for the Cleveland Rock stock was $5,000,000. P Corp., which is publicly traded, offered to purchase all of the Cleveland Rock. stock from Debby for $3,000,000. The purchase price was to be paid in the form of 12,000 shares of P Corp. worth $1,200,000 and $1,800,000 in cash. Debby's tax advisor, GMPK, CPA, LLC, advised Debby that a straightforward sale of the Cleveland Rock stock for $1,200,000 of P Stock and $1,800,000 of cash would not qualify as a reorganization under § 368 and that Debby could recognize a $2,000,000 loss of the sale of the Cleveland Rock stock. Debby never inquired about P Corp.'s plans for dealing with Cleveland Rock or Cleveland Rock's assets after the stock purchase and sale.

Unbeknownst to Debby, P Corp intended to merge Cleveland Rock into P Corp.'s preexisting wholly owned subsidiary, S Corp., which it did promptly after the acquisition. Upon audit of Debby's tax return the IRS asserted that Debby disposed of the Cleveland Rock stock in a forward triangular merger pursuant to § 368(a)(1)(A) and (a)(2)(D), and that Debby could not recognize the loss. Assess Debby's chances of prevailing in litigation on the issue.

3. The stock of T Corporation is publicly traded and widely held. T has only voting common stock outstanding. P Corporation acquired T Corporation in the following transactions, the plan for which was announced in advance. P Corporation made a tender offer in which it offered to pay two shares of P corporation voting common stock for each share of T stock, pursuant to which it acquired 60 percent of the outstanding T stock. Immediately thereafter, P formed a new wholly owned subsidiary, S Corporation, which it capitalized with cash and P voting common stock in equal amounts, followed by a merger of S Corporation into T Corporation. As a result of the merger of S Corporation into T Corporation, the T Corporation minority shareholders (who owned the 40 percent of T Corporation not acquired by P Corporation in the tender offer) surrendered all of their T stock and received one share of P voting common stock, plus an amount of cash of equal value to one share of P voting common stock, for each share of T Corporation stock surrendered. After the merger, P Corporation owned 100 percent of T Corporation. Do these transactions result in a tax-free reorganization? If so, what type?

E. TAX RESULTS TO THE PARTIES TO AN (A) REORGANIZATION

(1) SHAREHOLDERS AND SECURITY HOLDERS

1. Assume that all of the following *alternative* transactions occurred pursuant to a valid type (A) reorganization. A is a shareholder of T Corp., the acquired corporation, which is publicly traded. P Corp. is the acquiring corporation and also is publicly traded. In each case, what are the tax consequences to A? What is the amount of gain, if any, that A must recognize? What is A's basis in the stock or securities received?

   (a) A exchanged 300 shares of T stock, with a basis of $30 per share ($9,000 total) and fair market value of $12,000, for 150 shares of P common stock, having an aggregate fair market value of $15,000.

   (b) A exchanged 100 shares of T stock, with a basis of $45 per share ($4,500 total) and fair market value of $5,000, and 200 shares of T stock, with a basis of $22.50 per share ($4,500 total) and fair market value of $10,000, for 150 shares of P common stock, having an aggregate fair market value of $15,000.

(c) A exchanged 300 shares of T stock, with a basis of $30 per share ($9,000 total) and fair market value of $12,000, for 60 shares of P common stock, having a fair market value of $8,000, and 20 shares P nonvoting preferred stock, having a fair market value of $4,000.

(d) A exchanged 300 shares of T stock, with a basis of $30 per share ($9,000 total) and fair market value of $12,000, for 100 shares of P common stock, having an aggregate fair market value of $10,000, and $2,000 of cash.

(e) A exchanged 300 shares of T stock, with a basis of $30 per share ($9,000 total) and fair market value of $12,000, for 80 shares of P common stock, having an aggregate fair market value of $8,000 and $4,000 of cash.

(f) (1) A exchanged 100 shares of T stock, with a basis of $80 per share ($8,000 total) and fair market value of $4,000, and 200 shares of T stock, with a basis of $5 per share ($1,000 total) and fair market value of $8,000, for 150 shares of P common stock, having an aggregate fair market value of $9,000, and $3,000 of cash.

(2) A exchanged 100 shares of T preferred stock, with a basis of $80 per share ($8,000 total) and fair market value of $3,000, and 200 shares of T common stock, with a basis of $5 per share ($1,000 total) and fair market value of $9,000, for 133 shares of P common stock, having an aggregate fair market value of $8,000, and $4,000 of cash. The merger agreement provided that the holders of T common stock would receive P common stock and that the holders of T preferred stock would receive cash.

(g) (1) A exchanged 300 shares of T stock, with a basis of $30 per share ($9,000 total) and fair market value of $10,000, for 100 shares of P common stock, having an aggregate fair market value of $10,000, and options to purchase an additional 500 shares of P common stock at $92 per share. The 500 warrants have a fair market value of $1,000.

(2) What is A's tax treatment if the P warrants lapse before exercise?

(h) (1) A exchanged 300 shares of T stock, with a basis of $30 per share ($9,000 total) and fair market value of $12,000, for 60 shares of P common stock, having a fair market value of $8,000, and a P Corp. 20 year debt instrument, with a principal amount of $4,000 and a fair market value of $4,000.

(2) A exchanged 300 shares of T stock, with a basis of $30 per share ($9,000 total) and fair market value of $12,000, and a 20 year T debt

instrument having a redemption value and fair market value of $6,000, but which had a basis of only $5,400 because it was purchased at a market discount (not OID), for 50 shares of P common stock, having a fair market value of $9,000 and three P Corp. 20 year debt instruments, each of which had both a redemption value and fair market value of $3,000.

(3) A exchanged 300 shares of T stock, with a basis of $30 per share ($9,000 total) and fair market value of $12,000, for 60 shares of P common stock, having a fair market value of $8,000, and a P Corp. 20 year debt instrument, with a redemption value of $5,000, but which under the OID rules has a principal amount of only $4,000 because the stated interest rate is below the prevailing rate. How and when will A be taxed on any difference between the basis of the debt instrument and its redemption value?

2. B and C each own 200 shares of common stock of T Corporation. (T has a total of 400 outstanding shares.) Each of their blocks of stock has an aggregate basis of $50,000 and a fair market value of $200,000. In a valid type (A) reorganization, T Corporation was merged into P Corporation. Prior to the merger, P Corporation had outstanding 400 shares of common stock, which had an aggregate fair market value of $400,000. Each corporation had retained earnings and profits in excess of $300,000. Pursuant to the merger each of B and C received 120 shares of P common stock, having a fair market value of $120,000, and $80,000 in cash in exchange for their T stock.

(a) (1) What is the character of the gain recognized by B and C? Does it matter which corporation's cash reserves were used to pay B and C?

(2) Would your answer to question (a)(1) be different if B and C each received 150 shares of Y stock, having an aggregate fair market value of $150,000, and $50,000 of cash?

(3) Would your answer to question (a)(1) differ if P Corp. had $40,000 of accumulated earnings and profits and T Corp. had $30,000 of accumulated earnings and profits?

(b) What would be the consequences if B and C each received 150 shares of P common stock, having an aggregate fair market value of $150,000, and 50 shares of $1,000 par value nonvoting preferred stock, with limited rights to dividends and liquidation distributions?

3. F holds a publicly traded T Corporation 20 year debt instrument, which pays interest of 10% per annum, compounded semi-annually, was issued for $100,000 in cash, and has a redemption value of $100,000.

Pursuant to a valid type (A) reorganization in which T Corp. is merged into P Corp., F exchanges the T Corp. debt instrument for a publicly traded P Corp. debt instrument. What are the tax consequences to F and to P Corp. under the following alternative situations?

(a) The prevailing interest rate is 8% and the fair market value of F's T Corp. debt instrument is $125,000. F receives a P Corp. 20 year 8% P Corp. debt instrument having a redemption value of $125,000.

(b) The prevailing interest rate is 12.5% and the fair market value of F's T Corp. debt instrument is $80,000. F receives a P Corp. 12.5% debt instrument having a redemption value of $80,000.

(c) The prevailing interest rate is 10% and the fair market value of the T Corp. debt instrument, which has 20 years remaining until maturity, is $100,000. F receives a 20 year P Corp. debt instrument that pays no interest and has a redemption value of $704,000. The fair market value of the P debt instrument is $100,000. (The net present value of $704,000 due in 20 years, discounted at 10% per annum, compounded semi-annually, is $100,000.)

4. T Corp. is a closely held corporation that designs computer software. It has 1000 shares issued and outstanding. P Corp., which is publicly traded, proposes to acquire T Corp. in a stock-for-stock exchange, but the parties cannot agree on an exchange ratio. P Corp. has been trading on the NASDAQ system at between $18 and $22 a share during the last year. The parties agree that the T Corp. stock is worth between $1,000 and $2,000 per share, depending on the performance of a new data base management program introduced by T Corp. last week. The profitability of the new product should be clear in three or four years at the outside.

   How can the acquisition be structured to take into account the uncertain value of T Corporation? What are the relative tax and non-tax advantages and disadvantages of using a contingent stock arrangement versus an escrowed stock arrangement?

(2) TREATMENT OF THE CORPORATIONS PARTICIPATING IN AN (A) REORGANIZATION

1. P Corp. acquired T Corp. in a statutory merger in which the shareholders of T Corp. received P Corp. stock with a fair market value of $2,100,000 and $900,000 cash. T Corp.'s assets were as follows:

Asset	Adj. Basis	F.M.V.
Factory	$100,000	$600,000
Equipment	$300,000	$700,000
Inventory	$100,000	$800,000
Patent	$ 0	$900,000

How much gain must T Corp. recognize? What is P Corp.'s basis in the assets after the merger?

2. (a) In a statutory merger, P Corp. acquired real estate from T Corp. The real estate had a gross fair market value of $400, was subject to a mortgage of $100 and had a basis of $125. The sole shareholder of T Corp. had a $190 basis in her T Corp. stock and received 150 shares of P Corp. (fair market value of $300) in the merger. What are the tax consequences to the corporations?

   (b) Suppose the mortgage was $160. What are the tax consequences to the corporations?

SECTION 3. STOCK-FOR-STOCK ACQUISITIONS: TYPE (B) REORGANIZATIONS

1. In each of the following alternative transactions, P Corporation, the acquiring corporation, has exchanged its stock for stock of T Corporation, the acquired corporation. In each case determine whether, after taking into account the additional facts, a valid type (B) reorganization has occurred.

   (a) T Corp. had 1,000 shares of common stock outstanding. Prior to the transaction, P Corp. held no stock of T Corp.

      (1) P Corp. acquired 800 shares of T stock in exchange for 500 shares of P voting common stock.

      (2) P Corp. acquired 800 shares of T stock in exchange for 500 shares of P nonvoting common stock.

      (3) P Corp. acquired 800 shares of T stock in exchange for 500 shares of P voting preferred stock.

      (4) P Corp. acquired 800 shares of T stock in exchange for 500 shares of P preferred stock, which had no voting rights unless its cumulative, mandatory if earned, dividend had been missed for eight consecutive quarters; if the dividends were missed, the preferred stock had a right to elect a majority of the board of directors until the missed cumulative dividends had been paid.

(b) T Corp. had 100,000 shares of common stock and 1,000 shares of nonvoting preferred stock outstanding. The common stock had an aggregate value of $9,000,000; the preferred stock had a value of $1,000,000. Prior to the transaction, P Corp. held no stock of T Corp.

(1) P Corp. acquired all of the outstanding T Corp. common stock in exchange for its own voting common stock, but acquired none of the T Corp. preferred stock.

(2) P Corp. acquired 80,000 shares of T common stock for its voting common stock and all of the T nonvoting preferred stock in exchange for its own nonvoting preferred stock.

(3) P Corp. acquired 80,000 shares of T common stock for its voting common stock and 800 shares of the T nonvoting preferred stock in exchange for its own voting preferred stock.

(c) T Corp. has 1,000 shares of voting class A common stock, 3000 shares of class B nonvoting common stock, and 1,000 shares of nonvoting preferred stock outstanding. The class A common stock has an aggregate value of $900,000; the Class B common stock has an aggregate value of $2,000,000; and the preferred stock has an aggregate value of $3,000,000. P Corp. holds no stock of T Corp. but plans to acquire control. P Corp. will acquire all of the T Corp. class A common stock for its own voting common. It plans to issue additional voting common stock to acquire the minimum amount of the other two classes of stock required in order to qualify the transaction as a type (B) reorganization. How much of the T Corp. class B common and preferred stock must P Corp. acquire?

(d) T Corp. has 1000 shares of common stock outstanding. The value of a share of T common is $109. The value of a share of P common is $108. P acquires all of the T stock by offering one of its own shares of voting common stock, plus $1, for each share of T. Pursuant to the exchange offer, P issues 1000 shares of voting stock and pays the former T shareholders $1,000.

(e) T Corp. has 1000 shares of common stock outstanding. The value of a share of T common is $100. The value of a share of P common is $109. P acquires all of the T stock by offering 0.91743 of its own shares of voting common stock for each share of T, but fractional shares will not be issued. Cash will be paid in lieu of fractional shares. Pursuant to the exchange offer P gave each of the ten equal shareholders of T Corp. 91 shares of its voting stock and $81 cash in lieu of a 0.743 fractional share.

(f) T Corp. has 100,000 shares of voting common stock outstanding. The fair market value of a share of T is $100. P Corp. exchanges ten of its own shares, worth $10 each, plus options to purchase one of its shares for $9 anytime within the next year, worth $l, in exchange for each share of T. The purpose of the warrants was to make the exchange offer more attractive by offering a premium.

(g) Franklin, Gert, Harvey, Irene, and Jose are equal shareholders of T Corp. Each owns 20 shares. P Corp. acquires T Corp. by exchanging its voting stock for the T Corp. stock. Franklin, Gert, Harvey and Irene were willing to take P Corp. stock. Jose demanded and received cash.

(1) T corporation redeems all of Jose's stock immediately before the exchange. The exchange was conditional on redemption of Jose's stock in T.

(i) Does it matter if T Corp. borrows the money from P Corp. to pay Jose?

(ii) What if T Corp. borrowed the money to pay Jose from the Last National Bank and the loan was repaid by a capital contribution from P Corp. two years later?

(2) S Corp., an 80% controlled subsidiary of P Corp., purchases Jose's stock with funds obtained from operating revenues.

(3) Katia, an individual who owns 27% of the stock of P, purchases Jose's stock for cash obtained by selling portfolio securities.

(h) Lee owns an option to purchase 1000 shares of T Corp. stock at $8. Lee's basis in this option is $2,000, and the fair market value of the option is $5,000. In exchange for the option, P Corporation gives Lee an option to purchase 1000 shares of P Corp. stock at $14 per share. The fair market value of this option is $5,000. Does this affect the status of the reorganization?

2. (a) Alex, Bonnie, Colin, Danielle, and Earl each own 20 shares of T Corp. S Corp., a wholly owned subsidiary of P Corp., acquires T Corp. by exchanging P Corp. voting stock (which P Corp. contributed to S Corp. for this purpose) for the T Corp. stock.

(1) All of the T Corp. shareholders agree to take P Corp. stock.

(2) Alex, Bonnie, Colin, and Danielle are willing to take P Corp. stock. Earl demands cash. Z Corp., another wholly owned subsidiary of P Corp. buys Earl's stock.

(b) P Corp. owns all of the stock of X Corp., which in turn owns all of the stock of S Corp., i.e., S Corp is a second tier subsidiary of P Corp. S Corp. acquires T Corp. by exchanging P Corp. voting stock (which P Corp. contributed to X Corp., which in turn contributed the P stock to S Corp. for this purpose) for the T Corp. stock.

(c) P Corp. acquired all of the stock of T Corp. in exchange for P Corp. voting stock. Immediately following the acquisition, P Corp. transferred all of the T stock to its wholly owned subsidiary, X Corp., as a contribution to capital and immediately after that transfer, X Corp. transferred all of the T stock to its own wholly owned subsidiary, S Corp.

(d) The P Corp. affiliated group, which consists of P Corp. and its wholly owned subsidiaries, X Corp. and Y Corp., acquires the T Corp. stock in a transaction in which X Corp. acquires 60 percent of the outstanding T stock in exchange for P Corp. voting stock, which P Corp. contributed to X Corp. for this purpose, and Y Corp. acquires 40 percent of the outstanding T stock in exchange for P Corp. voting stock, which P Corp. contributed to Y Corp. for this purpose.

3. Twenty years ago P Corp. acquired 30 of the 100 authorized and outstanding shares of voting common stock of T Corp. T Corp. currently has outstanding 100 shares of voting common stock, including the 30 held by P Corp. P Corp. proposes to acquire additional shares of T Corp. in exchange for its own voting stock.

(a) How many shares of T Corp. common must it obtain in order for the acquisition to be a valid type (B) reorganization?'

(b) Suppose that the 70 shares of T Corp. not owned by P are held by ten different individuals, each of whom owns 7 shares. P Corp. individually negotiates with each shareholder and makes the following acquisitions of all of each shareholder's T Corp. shares for P Corp. voting stock.

Shareholder	*Date*
Arthur	1/ 5/2014
Bertha	2/ 6/2014
Cristobal	4/15/2014
Dolly	5/ 1/2014
Edouard	1/ 8/2015
Fay	3/17/2015
Gustav	4/ 1/2015
Hanna	4/14/2015
Ike	4/15/2016
Josephine	4/15/2018

Which of these acquisitions are part of a type (B) reorganization?

4. On April 15 of this year, Leviathan Corp. made a cash purchase of 1,000,000 shares of common stock of Bullseye, Inc. from the Stallmuckers Union Pension Trust Fund. Bullseye, Inc. is publicly traded, but the acquisition was privately negotiated. If Leviathan Corp. desires to acquire control of Bullseye in a stock-for-stock acquisition, how long must it wait before making a public exchange offer in order for the acquisition to qualify as a (B) reorganization? When the exchange is made, how much of the Bullseye common stock must Leviathan obtain in the stock-for-stock exchange in order to qualify the transaction as a type (B) reorganization?

5. Suppose that General Motors acquired Ford in a type (B) reorganization, and five years later, G.M. decided to sell all of its Ford stock to Toyota. How would G.M. determine its basis in the Ford stock in computing gain or loss on the sale? (Assume that no events in the five years between the acquisition and the sale affected the basis of the Ford stock in G.M.'s hands.)

SECTION 4. STOCK-FOR-ASSET ACQUISITIONS: TYPE (C) REORGANIZATIONS

1. In each of the following alternative transactions, T Corporation transfers assets to P Corporation in exchange for P Corporation stock (or other consideration stated in the question). In each case determine whether the transaction qualifies as a reorganization after taking into account the additional facts. If the transaction is not a reorganization, how is it treated?

   (a) T transfers all of its assets for P voting preferred stock, which T distributes to its shareholders in liquidation.

   (b) T transfers all of its assets for P nonvoting common stock, which T distributes to its shareholders in liquidation.

   (c) T transfers all of its assets for P voting common stock, which T continues to hold.

2. (a) T transfers all of its assets, having a fair market value of $1,000,000 and a basis of $800,000, for $700,000 of A voting common stock. P assumes $300,000 of T's debts secured by the assets. T liquidates.

   (b) T transfers all of its assets, having a fair market value of $1,000,000 and a basis of $200,000, for $700,000 of P voting common stock. P assumes $300,000 of T's debts secured by the assets. T liquidates.

(c) T transfers all of its assets, having a fair market value of $1,000,000 and a basis of $200,000, for $100,000 of P voting common stock. P assumes $900,000 of T's debts secured by the assets. T liquidates.

3. (a) T transfers all of its assets, having a fair market value of $1,000,000, for $800,000 of P voting common stock and $200,000 of cash. T has no debts. T liquidates.

   (b) T transfers all of its assets, having a fair market value of $1,000,000 for $700,000 of P voting common stock and $100,000 of cash. P assumes $200,000 of T's debts secured by the assets. T liquidates.

   (c) T transfers 90% of its assets, having a fair market value of $900,000 for $750,000 of P voting common stock and $150,000 of cash. T has no debts. T liquidates.

4. (a) T's assets consist of a factory, having a value of $700,000, subject to a mortgage of $200,000 and a warehouse, having a value of $300,000, also subject to a mortgage of $200,000. The factory is transferred to P for $500,000 of P stock and P takes the factory subject to the mortgage. T retains the warehouse, which it distributes to its shareholders in liquidation along with the P stock.

   (b) T's assets consist of a factory, having a value of $600,000, which is unencumbered and a warehouse, having a value of $400,000, subject to a mortgage of $390,000. The factory is transferred to P for $600,000 of P stock. T retains the warehouse, which it distributes to its shareholders in liquidation along with the P stock.

   (c) T's assets consist of a factory, having a value of $650,000 and undeveloped land held as an investment, having a value of $350,000. The factory is transferred to P for $650,000 of P stock. T retains the undeveloped land, which it distributes to its shareholders in liquidation along with the P stock.

5. P owns 70 of 100 shares of the stock of T; Omar owns the other 30 shares of T stock. T transfers all of its assets to P in exchange for 1000 shares of P stock, following which T liquidates, distributing 300 shares of P stock to Omar and 700 shares of P stock to P. The 700 shares of P stock transferred to T that were distributed to P in the liquidation are cancelled.

6. Marco owns 65 shares of T stock. Nana owns 35 shares of T stock. T's assets consist of a battery factory, having a value of $650,000, and a toxic waste dump site, having a value of $350,000. P wants to acquire T, including the factory, but not the toxic waste dump site. Marco is willing to accept P shares as consideration, but Nana is not. Pursuant

to a prearranged plan, the toxic waste dump site is distributed to Nana in redemption of Nana's 35 shares. Immediately thereafter, Marco exchanges the 65 remaining T shares for P voting stock. Within weeks, P liquidates T. Has a valid reorganization occurred?

7. (a) T transfers all of its assets, which had an aggregate basis of $600,000, to A for 10,000 shares of P stock, having a fair market value of $1,000,000. Pursuant to the plan of reorganization, P does not assume any debts of T. Instead, T distributes $100,000 worth of P stock to T's creditors in full satisfaction of all of its debts as part of T's liquidation. What are the tax consequences to T?

   (b) T transfers all of its assets, which had an aggregate basis of $600,000, to P for $1,000,000 of P voting stock. Pursuant to the plan of reorganization, P does not assume any debts of T. Instead, T sells 1,000 shares of A stock, worth $100,000, and pays the cash proceeds to its creditors in full satisfaction of all of its debts as part of T's liquidation. What are the tax consequences to T?

   (c) How do you explain the difference in results in (a) and (b)?

SECTION 5. TRIANGULAR REORGANIZATIONS

1. Ana, Bill, Claudette, Danny, and Erika each own 20 of the 100 issued and outstanding shares of voting common stock of T Corporation. T has no other stock outstanding. The fair market value of all 100 shares of T is $1,000,000. Each shareholder has a basis of $45,000. T Corporation is engaged in three businesses: it manufactures and sells the Bassamatic line of food processors; it packages and distributes frozen fish bait; and it operates a chain of fried squid fast food restaurants. P Corporation proposes to acquire T Corporation for stock and debt instruments, but for various non-tax reasons has decided that a direct asset acquisition is not desirable.

   Which of the following alternative transactions will qualify as a tax free reorganization? If the acquisition qualifies, is any boot involved? If there is boot, what is the amount of gain recognized by each shareholder of T?

   (a) T will merge into S Corporation, a newly formed subsidiary of P Corp. that has been capitalized with the consideration that will be transferred to the T shareholders. Each of the shareholders of T will receive the following consideration:

(1) 800 shares of voting common stock of P having a fair market value of $160,000 plus a 20-year P debt instrument having an issue price and fair market value of $40,000.

(2) 400 shares of voting common stock of P having a fair market value of $80,000 plus a 20-year P debt instrument having an issue price and fair market value of $120,000.

(3) 300 shares of voting common stock of P having a fair market value of $60,000 plus a 20-year P debt instrument having an issue price and fair market value of $140,000.

(4) 800 shares of nonvoting preferred stock of P having a fair market value of $160,000 plus a 20-year P debt instrument having an issue price and fair market value of $40,000.

(5) 800 shares of voting common stock of P having a fair market value of $160,000 plus 200 shares of nonvoting preferred stock of S having a fair market value of $40,000.

(6) 800 shares of voting common stock of P having a fair market value of $160,000 plus a 20-year S debt instrument having an issue price and fair market value of $40,000.

(7) Ana and Bill each will receive 1,000 shares of voting common stock of P, worth $200 per share, while Claudette, Danny, and Erika each will receive $200,000 of cash.

(b)(1) T will sell the frozen fish bait business for $200,000 and will use the proceeds to redeem all of Erika's stock. Following the redemption, T will merge into S. Ana, Bill, Claudette, and Danny each will receive 400 shares of P stock having a value of $80,000 and $120,000 of P debt instruments. (Aggregate consideration paid to Ana, Bill, Claudette, and Danny is $320,000 in stock and $480,000 in debt instruments.)

(2) T will sell publicly traded portfolio stock investments that it accumulated in excess of working capital needs for $100,000 and will use the proceeds to redeem one-half of Erika's stock. Following the redemption, T will merge into S. Ana, Bill, Claudette, and Danny each will receive 400 shares of P stock having a value of $80,000 and $120,000 of P debt instruments. Erika will receive 200 shares of P stock having a value of $40,000 and $60,000 of P debt instruments. (Aggregate consideration paid to Ana, Bill, Claudette, Danny and Erika in the merger is $360,000 in stock and $540,000 in debt instruments.)

(c)(1) Assume the same basic facts as in (a), but last year, Ana, Bill, and Claudette each sold their shares of T to S Corp. for $200,000 cash. In the current year, T Corp. merged into S Corp. with Danny and Erika each receiving only stock of P Corp. worth $200,000.

(2) What if last year, Ana, Bill, Claudette, Danny, and Erika each sold 14 of their 20 shares of T to S Corp. for $140,000 cash. In the current year, T Corp. merged into S Corp. and Ana, Bill, Claudette, Danny, and Erika each received only stock of P Corp. worth $60,000 for their remaining 6 shares of T.

(d) Assume the same basic facts as in (a), but that T Corp. had outstanding options held by Fred to purchase T stock. Fred's options entitled Fred to purchase 20 shares of T stock for $200,000.

(1) What are the consequences of Fred being issued an option to purchase 200 shares of P stock for $200,000 in consideration of cancellation of Fred's options to purchase T Corp. stock?

(2) What are the consequences Fred being paid cash to surrender the options on T stock?

2. Assume the same facts as in (a)(1), except that P Corp owns 300 shares of S Corp. voting common stock (all of the S Corp. voting stock), and S Corp. also has outstanding 100 shares of preferred stock.

(a) The preferred stock is nonvoting and all 100 shares of S Corp. nonvoting preferred stock are held by the Buggy Whip Manufacturer's Union Pension Trust Fund.

(b) The preferred stock is voting stock and only 75 shares of the S Corp. voting preferred stock held are by the Buggy Whip Manufacturer's Union Pension Trust Fund; P Corp. holds 25 shares of the S Corp. voting preferred stock.

3. (a) Assume the same facts as in (a)(1). P Corp. owns 100 percent of the stock of X Corp., which in turn owns 100 percent of the stock of S Corp. T Corp. is merged into S Corp. and the shareholders of T receive voting common stock of P Corp.

(b) P Corp. owns 100 percent of the stock of both X Corp. and S Corp. T Corp. is merged into S Corp. and the shareholders of T receive voting common stock of P Corp. Following the merger P Corp, transfers the stock of S Corp. to X Corp.

(c) P Corp. owns 100 percent of the stock of X Corp., which in turn owns 100 percent of the membership units in S LLC. T Corp. is merged into S LLC and the shareholders of T receive voting common stock of P Corp.

4. The stock of T Corporation is publicly traded and widely held. T has only voting common stock outstanding. P Corporation acquired T Corporation in the following transactions, the plan for which was announced in advance. P Corporation acquired 51 percent of the outstanding T stock pursuant to a tender offer in which it paid cash. Immediately thereafter, P formed a new wholly owned subsidiary, S Corporation, which it capitalized with P nonvoting preferred stock, followed by a merger of T Corporation into S Corporation. As a result of the merger of T Corporation into S Corporation, the T Corporation minority shareholders (who owned the 49 percent of T Corporation not acquired by P Corporation in the tender offer) surrendered all of their T stock and received P nonvoting preferred stock in exchange for their T Corporation stock. Do these transactions result in a tax-free forward triangular merger?

5. T Corp. merged into S Corp., a newly formed subsidiary of P Corp. that had been capitalized with $1,000 plus 5,000 shares of P Corp. common stock having an aggregate fair market value of $1,000,000. T Corp.'s assets had a fair market value of $1,300,000 and a basis of $400,000. Pursuant to the merger, S Corp. assumed $300,000 of T Corp.'s debts secured by the assets. Each of the shareholders of T received 1,000 of the P Corp. shares held by S Corp. immediately before the merger.

(a) What is P's basis for its S stock immediately after the merger?

(b)(1) What if T Corp.'s debts were $500,000?

(2) Would your answer change if the P Corp. affiliated group filed a consolidated return?

6. Ana, Bill, Claudette, Danny, and Erika each own 20 of the 100 issued and outstanding shares of voting common stock of T Corporation. T has no other stock outstanding. The fair market value of all 100 shares of T is $1,000,000. Each shareholder has a basis of $45,000. T Corporation is engaged in three businesses: it manufactures and sells the Bassamatic line of food processors; it packages and distributes frozen fish bait; and it operates a chain of fried squid fast food restaurants. P Corporation proposes to acquire T Corporation for stock and debt instruments, but for various non-tax reasons has decided that a direct asset acquisition is not desirable. (These are the same basic facts as in the introductory paragraphs to question 1.)

(a) P Corp. will form a new wholly owned subsidiary, S Corp., which will merge into T Corp. Under the terms of the merger, P's stock in S will be exchanged for T stock, and each of the shareholders of T will receive the following alternative consideration in exchange for their T stock:

(1) 800 shares of voting common stock of P having a fair market value of $160,000 plus a 20-year P debt instrument having an issue price and fair market value of $40,000.

(2) 750 shares of voting common stock of P having a fair market value of $150,000 plus a 20-year P debt instrument having an issue price and fair market value of $50,000.

(3) 1000 shares of nonvoting common stock of P having a fair market value of $200,000.

(4) 800 shares of voting preferred stock of P having a fair market value of $160,000 plus a 20-year P debt instrument having an issue price and fair market value of $40,000.

(5) 800 shares of voting common stock of P having a fair market value of $160,000 plus 200 shares of nonvoting preferred stock of T having a fair market value of $40,000.

(b) Assume the same facts as in question 6(a)(1) except that T Corporation also has outstanding 100 shares of nonvoting preferred stock, which are held by the State of Utopia Public Employees' Retirement Pension Trust Fund. Must the nonvoting preferred stock of T (which is the surviving corporation) be surrendered in exchange for P stock in order to qualify as a reorganization?

(c) Assume the basic facts as in question 6(a)(1), but Erika votes against the merger (which is adopted by a 80-20 vote of T's shares). Erika exercises state law dissenters' rights to be paid in cash. S is merged into T and Ana, Bill, Claudette, and Danny each receive 999 shares of voting stock of P, worth $199,800, and $200 cash.(Aggregate consideration paid to Ana, Bill, Claudette, and Danny is $799,200 in stock and $800 in cash.)

(1) Erika is paid out of T's cash balances existing before the merger.

(2) Erika is paid by T after the merger, with cash contributed by P.

7. Assume the same basic facts as in the introductory paragraphs to question 6. S Corp. is an existing wholly owned subsidiary of P Corporation. S was organized 15 years ago and is engaged in the

manufacture of fishing lures. S will be merged into T and each of the shareholders of T will receive 1,000 shares of voting stock of P, having a fair market value of $200,000. Are the following alternative transactions tax-free?

(a) Following the merger, T will sell the fishing lure business to Y Corp. for $1,000,000 and the proceeds will be used to expand the Bassamatic business.

(b) Following the merger, T will sell the frozen fish bait business and the fried squid business for $600,000 and use the proceeds to expand the fishing lure business.

(c) Following the merger, T will sell the frozen fish bait business and the fried squid business for $600,000 and use the proceeds to expand the Bassamatic business.

8. (a) Assume the same basic facts as in the introductory paragraphs to question 6. Three years ago, P purchased the 40 shares of T stock owned by Ana and Bill for $400,000, thus holding 40 percent of the outstanding T stock. Last year, S Corp., a newly formed subsidiary of P, was merged into T Corp. As a result of the merger, P's stock of S Corp. was canceled and Claudette, Danny, and Erika each received voting common stock of P Corp. worth $200,000 ($600,000 in the aggregate). P's 40 shares of T Corp. thereby became 100 percent of the outstanding stock of T. What are the tax results to the parties?

   (b) Three years ago, P purchased the 20 shares of T stock owned by Ana for $200,000, thus holding 20 percent of the outstanding T stock. Last year, S Corp., a newly formed subsidiary of P, was merged into T Corp. As a result of the merger, P's stock of S Corp. was canceled and Bill, Claudette, Danny, and Erika each received voting common stock of P Corp. worth $200,000 ($800,000 in the aggregate). P's 20 shares of T thereby became 100 percent of the outstanding stock of T. What are the tax results to the parties?

9. (a) P Corp. owns 100 percent of the stock of X Corp., which in turn owns 100 percent of the stock of S Corp. S Corp. is merged into T Corp. and the shareholders of T receive voting common stock of P Corp. What are the tax results to the parties?

   (b) P Corp. owns 100 percent of the stock of both X Corp. and S Corp. S Corp. is merged into T Corp. and the shareholders of T receive voting common stock of P Corp. Following the merger P Corp, transfers the stock of T Corp. to X Corp.

(c) P Corp. owns 100 percent of the stock of X Corp., which in turn owns 100 percent of S LLC, a special purpose vehicle organized solely for the purpose of the acquisition and which was capitalized only with the consideration to be received by the T shareholders in the merger. S LLC is merged into T Corp. and the shareholders of T receive voting common stock of P Corp.

10. P Corp. formed a wholly owned subsidiary, S Corp., for the purpose of acquiring T Corp. in a reverse triangular merger. P Corp. capitalized S Corp. with 100 shares of voting common stock of P Corp. that would be the consideration provided to the sole shareholder of T Corp. in the merger, and P Corp. received one share of S Corp. stock. T Corp.'s sole asset was a parcel of land with a basis of $100,000, subject to mortgage of $95,000. T Corp.'s sole shareholder, Franklin, had a basis of $70,000 in the T Corp. stock. In the merger of S Corp. into T Corp., Franklin received the 100 shares of P Corp. voting common stock P held by S Corp., and P Corp.'s one share of S Corp. was converted into the only outstanding share of T Corp. What is P Corp.'s basis in its T Corp. stock after the reverse triangular merger?

SECTION 6. ACQUISITIVE TYPE (D) REORGANIZATIONS

1. Alberto, Beryl, Chris, and Debby each owned 25 of the 100 outstanding shares of common stock of Cyclone Fence Corp. Cyclone Fence Corp. sold all of its assets to Tropical Landscapers, Inc. in exchange for 200 shares of voting common stock of Tropical Landscapers, worth $800,000 and $800,000 in cash. After the asset sale, Cyclone Fence Corp. liquidated, distributing the Tropical Landscapers stock and cash pro rata to Alberto, Beryl, Chris, and Debby. Is the acquisition of Cyclone Fence Corp. by Tropical Landscapers a reorganization under the following alternative fact patterns?

(a) Before the acquisition, Tropical Landscapers, Inc. had 200 shares of voting common stock outstanding, which was owned equally by Earl and Fiona (100 shares each).

(b) Before the acquisition, Tropical Landscapers, Inc. had 210 shares of voting common stock outstanding, which was owned equally by Earl, Fiona, and Gaston (70 shares each).

(c) Before the acquisition, Tropical Landscapers, Inc. had 210 shares of voting common stock outstanding, which was owned equally by Debby, Earl, and Fiona (70 shares each).

(d) Before the acquisition, Tropical Landscapers, Inc. had had 200 shares of voting common stock outstanding, which was owned equally by Earl and Fiona (100 shares each), and Hermine held all 100 shares of issued and outstanding nonvoting limited and preferred stock of Tropical Landscapers, Inc., which had a par value and fair market value of $2,000,000.

2. (a) X Corp. owned all the stock of both Y Corp. and Z Corp. Y Corp. owned Blackacre and Whiteacre. Blackacre had a fair market value of $2,000,000 and a basis of $500,000. Whiteacre had a fair market value of $2,000,000 and a basis of $3,500,000. Y Corp. sold Blackacre and Whiteacre to Z Corp. for $4,000,000 in cash and liquidated. What is the basis of each of Blackacre and Whiteacre to Z Corp?

   (b) Would your answer differ if immediately after the sale acquisition of Blackacre and Whiteacre by Z Corp., Z Corp. transferred the properties to its wholly owned subsidiary, S Corp., as a contribution to capital?

3. Ida and Joaquin are equal shareholders of Windward Properties, Inc. Each of them has a $100,000 basis in the stock of Windward Properties. Windward Properties' assets consist of a parcel of land with a fair market value of $10,000 and a basis of $70,000 and cash of $30,000. Ida and Joaquin have a plan to liquidate Windward Properties, then contribute the land to a newly formed corporation, Leeward Properties, owned equally by them and sell the stock of Leeward Properties to Kate. What are the tax consequences of this transaction?

PART VI

NONACQUISITIVE REORGANIZATIONS

CHAPTER 22

SINGLE CORPORATION REORGANIZATIONS

SECTION 2. RECAPITALIZATIONS

1. Louisville Coal and Oil Co., Inc. (LCO), which is publicly traded, has 1,000,000 shares of no par common stock outstanding. LCO also has outstanding 10,000 shares of $100 par, 5% preferred stock. LCO's indebtedness consists of: (1) $10,000,000 principal amount 6% debt instruments due in 2040, which were issued for their face amount; and (2) $8,000,000 in bank loans.

   To what extent do any of the following proposed transactions qualify as a recapitalization? Do any shareholders or creditors of LCO, or LCO itself, nevertheless recognize any gain or loss even though the transaction may qualify as a recapitalization?

(a) Common shareholders could exchange existing voting common stock for newly created Class B common stock at the ratio of twelve shares of new class B nonvoting common stock for every ten shares of voting common stock surrendered. With the exception of voting privileges, the class B common stock would be identical to the class A common stock.

(b)(1) Common shareholders could exchange up to one-half of their existing common stock for authorized but unissued nonvoting preferred stock at the exchange rate of five shares of common for one share of nonvoting preferred stock.

(2) Would your answer differ if the preferred stock were sinking fund preferred stock redeemable 25 years after issuance?

(c) All common shares would be converted into newly created Class A common stock and newly created Class B preferred stock at the exchange rate of one share of old common in exchange for one share of newly issued voting common and one share of newly issued nonvoting preferred stock.

(d) Common shareholders could elect to surrender up to 10 percent of their shares of LCO voting common stock in exchange for subordinated debt instruments of LCO bearing interest at two percentage points over the prime rate, which would be due in 2050.

(e) Preferred shareholders could elect to convert their preferred stock into common stock at the ratio of six shares of common for every share of preferred.

(1) Does the trading price of the common matter? Assume alternatively that the common is trading for $18 per share, $20 per share, and $22 per share.

(2) Would your answer differ if the preferred stock had $10 of dividends in arrears?

(f) The outstanding $1,000 debt instruments are currently trading for $680. LCO's debt instrument holders could exchange their debt instruments on the following alternative terms:

(1) Ten old debt instruments for seven new $1,000 debt instruments bearing interest two percentage points over the prime rate at the time of issuance. LCO expects the new debt instruments would trade for their face amount.

(2) Debt instrument holders could exchange a $1,000 debt instrument for 36 shares of LCO common stock, which is expected to be trading at $20 per share on the exchange date. Thus, each bondholder would receive stock worth $720 for each $1,000 bond worth $680.

(3) Would your answers be affected if the recapitalization were pursuant to Chapter 11 of the Bankruptcy Act?

(g) The Last National Bank, which holds a $2,000,000 demand note, with $500,000 of interest in arrears, would exchange the note for 90,000 shares of LCO common stock, which is currently trading at $20 per share.

SECTION 3. CHANGE IN IDENTITY, FORM, OF PLACE OF ORGANIZATION: TYPE (F) REORGANIZATIONS

1. Pig Pit Barbecue Corp., a Kentucky corporation, originally operated a small barbecue restaurant in Owensboro, Kentucky. Due to the phenomenal success of its sauce recipe, Pig Pit has come to enjoy a national reputation, and its founder, Barbecue Bob, wants to take the corporation public. In preparation for an initial public offering, corporate counsel has advised Bob to "reincorporate" in Delaware.

   (a) How should the "reincorporation" be structured to assure the reincorporation is a type (F) reorganization?

   (b) Can the reincorporation be a type (F) reorganization if Pig Pit currently also has outstanding a class of preferred stock, held by Bob's cousin Gerry, who provided financing to expand the kitchen a few years ago, and in connection with the moving the state of incorporation from Kentucky to Delaware, Bob and Gerry have agreed that Gerry's preferred stock would be converted into common stock?

   (c) Can the reincorporation be a type (F) reorganization if Bob owned 60 percent of the common stock of Pig Pit and Bob's cousin Gerry owned 40 percent of the common stock, and in connection with the moving the state of incorporation from Kentucky to Delaware, Bob and Gerry have agreed that Gerry's common stock would be redeemed?

2. Earlier this year, P Corp. acquired 100 percent of the stock of S Corp. in a reverse triangular merger. Because S Corp. is engaged in the same line of business as X Corp., another wholly owned subsidiary of P Corp., P Corp. wants to merge S Corp. into X Corp.

   (a) Will the merger be tax free? Will it be a Type (F) reorganization?

(b) Would the merger be tax free if X Corp. were a shell and the purpose of the merger was to change the state of incorporation of the S Corp. business? Would it be a Type (F) reorganization?

CHAPTER 23

CORPORATE DIVISIONS: SPIN-OFFS, SPLIT-OFFS, AND SPLIT-UPS

SECTION 1. CORPORATE DIVISIONS: GENERAL RULES

1. (a) D Corp. was engaged in the production and sale of both computer hardware and computer software. D Corp. transferred all of the assets of its computer software business to a newly formed wholly-owned subsidiary, C Corp., and immediately thereafter, pursuant to a prearranged plan, distributed all of the stock of C Corp. pro rata to the D Corp. shareholders. Is it possible for these transactions to qualify for nonrecognition treatment, or must D Corp. recognize gain and its shareholders recognize dividend income?

   (b) D Corp. was engaged in the production and sale of computer hardware. D Corp.'s wholly-owned subsidiary, C Corp., was engaged in the production and sale of computer software. The stock of D Corp. was owned equally by Alma, Boris, and Christina. D Corp. distributed the stock of C Corp. to Alma in redemption of all of Alma's stock in D Corp. Is it possible for the distribution to qualify for nonrecognition treatment, or must either or both of D Corp. and Alma recognize gain?

   (c) D Corp. was engaged in the construction business. The stock of D Corp. was owned equally by Dolores and Enrique. D Corp transferred one-half of the assets of its construction business to a newly formed wholly owned subsidiary, C Corp., and immediately thereafter, pursuant to a prearranged plan, distributed all of the stock of C Corp. to Dolores, in complete redemption of all of her stock of D Corp. Is it possible for these transactions to qualify for nonrecognition treatment, or must either or both of D Corp. and Dolores recognize gain?

   (d) D Corp. was engaged in the manufacture and sale of cellular telephones. D Corp.'s wholly-owned subsidiary, C Corp. was engaged in the manufacture and sale of radios. The 90 shares of stock of D Corp. were owned equally by Felicia, Guillermo, and Hilda (30 shares each). D Corp distributed all of the stock of C Corp. to Felicia in redemption of one-tenth of her stock of her stock of D Corp., i.e., 3 shares. Is it possible for the distribution to qualify for nonrecognition treatment, or must either or both of D Corp. and Felicia recognize gain?

2. (a) Aletta and Bud each own 50 shares of stock of X Corp., which is a holding company that does not directly engage in any business. X Corp. owns all of the stock of both Y Corp. and Z Corp. Y Corp. manufactures gizmos and Z Corp. manufactures gadgets. X Corp. liquidates and distributes all of the stock of Y Corp. to Aletta and all of the stock of Z Corp. to Bud. Is it possible for the distribution to qualify for nonrecognition treatment, or must X Corp., Aletta, and Bud recognize gain?

   (b)(1) Suppose instead that Aletta and Bud each owned 50 shares of stock of both Y Corp. and Z Corp. (and X Corp. did not initially exist). Aletta and Bud formed X Corp. by contributing their stock of both Y Corp. and Z Corp. to X Corp. solely in exchange for X Corp. stock. Six months later, pursuant to a prearranged plan, X Corp. liquidated and distributed all of the stock of Y Corp. to Aletta and all of the stock of Z Corp. to Bud. Is it possible for the transactions to qualify for nonrecognition treatment, or must X Corp., Aletta, and Bud recognize gain?

   (2) Would your answer change if there were no prearranged plan to liquidate X Corp. but the decision to liquidate X Corp. was reached 3 years later when Aletta and Bud had a falling-out over how best to conduct the businesses?

3. Carlotta owned 70 out of the 90 shares of X Corp.; Daniel owned the other 20 shares of X Corp. X Corp. owned 75 out of 100 shares of Y Corp. Carlotta owned the other 25 shares of Y Corp. Carlotta transferred her 25 shares of Y Corp. to X Corp. in exchange for 10 additional shares of X Corp. (Assume that the 25 shares of Y Corp. are equal in value to the to 10 additional shares of X Corp.) Thereafter, X Corp. distributed all of the stock of Y Corp. to Carlotta and Daniel pro rata. Is it possible for these transactions to qualify for nonrecognition treatment, or must X Corp. recognize gain and Carlotta and Daniel recognize dividend income?

SECTION 2. "ACTIVE CONDUCT OF A TRADE OR BUSINESS," "DEVICE," AND OTHER LIMITATIONS

B. ACTIVE CONDUCT OF A TRADE OR BUSINESS

1. Mullet Corp. is engaged in the processing and sale of frozen seafood products. Its packing plant is owned by its wholly owned subsidiary, Seashell Corp. Mullet proposes to distribute all the stock of Seashell

Corp. to its shareholders, pro rata. Consider whether the corporate division would meet the "active business" test of § 355 given the following alternative additional facts.

(a) Seashell Corp. operates the packing plant using its employees, and sells the packaged seafood to Mullet, which markets it.

(b) Seashell Corp. leases the packing plant to Mullet, which operates it with Mullet employees. Seashell has no assets other than the packing plant and a bank account.

(c)(1) Seashell's real estate holdings include not only the packing plant, which it leases to Mullet, but a restaurant that it leases to Tuna Corp., which is unrelated to Seashell, Mullet, or Mullet's shareholders.

(2) Seashell's real estate holdings include not only the packing plant and restaurant, but a large marina that it leases to Poseidon Corp., which is unrelated to Seashell, Mullet, or Mullet's shareholders.

(d) Seashell's assets include the packing plant, which it leases to Mullet, and a sushi bar restaurant that it operates.

2. SweatSox Corp., which is equally owned by Calvin and Dora, sells athletic wear at retail. Until four years ago, its operations were confined to the Eastern Seaboard, where it had over 100 stores from Maine to Florida. Four years ago, SweatSox began retail sales on the West Coast, and in the past four years it has opened 50 stores from Southern California to Seattle. Consider whether the corporate division would meet the "active business" test of § 355 given the following alternative additional facts.

(a) SweatSox proposes to transfer the California and Florida stores to a new subsidiary, SunshineSports Corp., and then to distribute all of the SunshineSports Corp. stock to Calvin in complete redemption of his stock in SweatSox.

(b) SweatSox Corp. proposes to transfer the West Coast stores to a new subsidiary, LeftCoast, Inc., and then to distribute all of the LeftCoast, Inc., stock to Dora in complete redemption of her stock in SweatSox.

3. Mako Corp. is engaged in the business of manufacturing scuba diving equipment. Frostbite Corp., a wholly owned subsidiary of Mako, is engaged in the business of manufacturing snowmobiles. Except as provided in the individual questions, each business has been conducted for 6 years. Mako distributes the stock of Frostbite pro rata to its

shareholders. Does the distribution qualify under the active business test, if:

(a) Frostbite purchased the snowmobile business from an unrelated seller four years ago?

(b) Frostbite purchased the snowmobile business from an unrelated seller six years ago?

(c) Frostbite purchased the snowmobile business from Icicle Corp., another wholly owned subsidiary of Mako, four years ago?

(d) Frostbite Corp. itself was acquired by Mako 3 years ago in a reverse triangular merger (which qualified under § 368(a)(2)(E)) in which no boot was distributed?

(e) Frostbite was acquired 3 years ago in a reverse triangular merger (which qualified under § 368(a)(2)(E)) in which 10 percent of the consideration was cash?

(f) Frostbite was formed four years ago (in a § 351 transaction) by Mako, which contributed the snowmobile business, which Mako previously had operated as a division for three years? In the transaction to form Frostbite, Mako transferred assets with a fair market value of $5,000,000 and a basis of $1,000,000, subject to $1,500,000 of liabilities that were assumed by Frostbite.

(g) Frostbite was formed ten years ago as a joint venture with Stinkpot Corp, a manufacturer of power boats. Mako and Stinkpot each owned 50 percent of the stock until three years ago. Three years ago, Frostbite redeemed all of Stinkpots's stock, leaving Mako as the sole shareholder.

4. Blueberry Corp. is engaged in the business of wireless handheld e-mail devices. Tunes Corp., a wholly owned subsidiary of Blueberry, is engaged in the business of manufacturing portable media players. Both businesses have been conducted for 6 years. One-half the stock of Blueberry is owned by Peaches Corp. and the other one-half is owned by MacroSoft, Inc. Peaches and Macrosoft are wholly-owned subsidiaries of Dredmon Corp. Peaches and Macrosoft purchased their stock of Blueberry three years ago. Blueberry distributes the stock of Tunes pro rata to Peaches and Macrosoft. Does the distribution qualify under the active business test?

5. Point-N-Click Corp. is engaged in the retail camera sales business. Until three years ago, Point-N-Click's business was confined to consumer-grade digital cameras sold through an internet website.

Three years ago, Point-N-Click opened several retail stores catering to professional photographers, in which it sold high-end digital cameras and film cameras. The management of Point-N-Click believes that the retail stores catering to professional photographers would perform better if ownership were separated from the internet based business catering to consumers. The plan is to transfer the retail stores to a newly formed subsidiary, Derrogotype, and then to spin-off Derrogotype to the Point-N-Click shareholders. Does the distribution qualify under the active business test?

C. THE "DEVICE" LIMITATION

1. Erick and Flossie each own 50 shares of Mullet Corp., which has 100 shares outstanding. Mullet Corp. is engaged in the frozen seafood and fish bait businesses. Squid Corp., a wholly owned subsidiary of Mullet, operates a sushi bar restaurant. All of the business have been owned and conducted by the respective corporations for 6 years. Consider whether each of the following corporate divisions would meet the "device" test of § 355.

   (a) Mullet distributes the stock of Squid to Erick and Flossie pro rata.

   (b) Mullet distributes the stock of Squid to Flossie in redemption of all of her Mullet stock.

   (c) Mullet distributes the stock of Squid to Flossie in redemption of 25 shares of her Mullet stock.

   (d) Mullet distributes the stock of Squid to Flossie in redemption of 5 shares of her Mullet stock.

   (e) Mullet distributes all of the stock of Squid to Flossie in redemption of half of her Mullet stock and simultaneously redeems half of Erick's Mullet stock for cash.

   (f) Mullet distributes the stock of Squid to Flossie in redemption of all of her Mullet stock, but immediately before the distribution, Mullet contributes $500,000 cash to Squid (thereby increasing the fair market value of the Squid stock from $1,500,000 to $2,000,000).

   (g) Mullet distributes the stock of Squid to Flossie in redemption of all of her Mullet stock, but immediately before the distribution, Mullet contributes operating assets comprising its fish bait division, worth $500,000, to Squid

2. Suphuric Electric Power Corp. is a public utility engaged in the business of generating electric power. Its wholly owned subsidiary,

Carboniferous Corp. operates a coal mine. If Suphuric Electric Power Corp. distributes all of the stock of Carboniferous Corp. pro rata to the Suphuric Electric Power shareholders, are the active business and device tests met under the following circumstances?

(a) Carboniferous has been selling, and will continue to sell all of the output of its coal mine to Suphuric Electric Power pursuant to a long-term contract signed two years ago, and which runs for eight more years.

(b) Carboniferous sells its coal to various customers and for the past few years has been selling approximately 25 percent of its output to Suphuric Electric Power. Carboniferous is expected to continue to operate in the same manner after the distribution.

3. National Telephone & Telegraph Co. (NT&T), the stock of which is publicly traded, is engaged in three lines of business: (1) it provides cellular telephone service in portions of 46 states; (2) it provides land-line long distance telephone service nationwide; and (3) it manufactures personal computers. NT&T proposes to spin-off its personal computer business by forming a new subsidiary, Citrus Computer Corp., which will be distributed to NT&T's shareholders. Citrus Computer Corp. will start public trading on NASDAQ immediately after the spin-off. Will this transaction be a device?

4. Worldwide Waste Management Corp. has approached the board of directors of Bay State By-Products Corp. with an offer to acquire Bay State, but Worldwide does not want to acquire Bay State's controlled subsidiary, Toxic Trucking, Inc. Worldwide and Bay State have devised the following plan. Bay State will distribute Toxic to its shareholders pro rata. Following the distribution, Bay State will be merged into Worldwide in a merger in which the Bay State shareholders will receive only Worldwide common stock (with cash for fractional shares). Is the transaction a "device?" Might it fail to qualify under § 355 for some other reason?

D. THE BUSINESS PURPOSE REQUIREMENT

1. Julio and Karina own 50 percent of Mullet Corp. Mullet Corp. is engaged in the frozen fish bait business and the operation of a sushi bar restaurant. Each business has been conducted for 6 years. Consider whether each of the following corporate divisions would meet the "business purpose" test of § 355.

   (a) Julio is more interested in operating a sushi bar and Karina is more interested in operating a fish bait business. To this end, Mullet transfers the sushi bar business to a new wholly owned subsidiary,

Squid Corp., and Mullet distributes all of the Squid stock to Julio in exchange for his Mullet stock.

(b) Julio and Karina have decided that it would be prudent to separate the fish bait business from the risks of the sushi bar business. To this end, Mullet transfers the sushi bar business to a new wholly owned subsidiary, Squid Corp., and Mullet distributes all of the Squid stock pro rata to Julio and Karina.

2. George, a licensed civil engineer, owns 100% of the stock of Goethals Corporation, which conducts two related but separate businesses, a civil engineering consulting business and a construction business. Dalila is a brilliant and valued employee in the construction business. Dalila has received an offer from another company that includes an equity interest. To induce Dalila to stay, George proposes to cause Goethals Corporation to drop the construction business into a newly formed subsidiary, Bricks & Mortar, Inc., which will be spun-off to George, following which Dalila will receive a bonus from Bricks & Mortar in the form of stock that will total 25 percent of the then outstanding stock and an option to purchase enough additional shares from Bricks & Mortar to give Dalila a 50 percent interest. The reason for the transaction is to provide Dalila an equity interest in the Bricks & Mortar division, in which she is employed, but not in the civil engineering business (Dalila is not a licensed civil engineer). Does this transaction satisfy the business purpose requirement? Does it matter whether or not applicable state law allows individuals who are not licensed as civil engineers to own stock in a corporation that performs civil engineering consulting services?

3. (a) Kenneth owns 100 percent of the stock of Barleycorn Corp., which is engaged in the whiskey distilling and natural whole grain bread baking businesses. Each business has been conducted for over 20 years. Kenneth is 60 years old and as part of his estate planning wants to transfer his business to his children, Linda and Max. Linda wants to operate the bread baking business, and Max wants to operate the whiskey distilling business. To this end, Barleycorn Corp. plans to transfer the bread baking business to a new wholly owned subsidiary, Wheatberry Corp., all of the stock of which will be distributed to Kenneth. As soon as possible thereafter, Kenneth will transfer the Wheatberry stock to Linda and the Barleycorn stock to Max. Does this transaction meet the device and business purpose tests of § 355?

   (b) Suppose that after the distribution of Wheatberry to Kenneth but before he could transfer the stock of Wheatberry and Barleycorn and to Linda and Max, both Linda and Max unexpectedly died in an accident. As a result, Kenneth was left owning and operating both Wheatberry and Barleycorn. Is your answer affected?

SECTION 3. DISTRIBUTION OF "CONTROL" AND CONTINUITY OF INTEREST REQUIREMENTS

1. D Corporation, which is publicly traded, owned all of the stock of C Corporation. To increase stock values, D Corporation plans to spin-off C Corporation, which would also become publicly traded. Simultaneously, D desires to raise some additional cash. To this end, D Corporation proposes to distribute 80 percent of the stock of C Corporation to the D Corporation shareholders pro rata, and simultaneously to distribute pro rata to its shareholders options to purchase the remaining 20 percent of the stock of C Corporation at fair market value. Will the distribution qualify under § 355?

2. Cayo Hueso Corp. has approached the board of directors of Margaritaville Corp. with an offer to acquire Margaritaville, except it does not want to acquire Margaritaville's controlled subsidiary, Conch Corp. Cayo Hueso and Margaritaville have devised the following plan. Margaritaville will distribute Conch to its shareholders pro rata. (Assume that this distribution could have qualified under § 355 if nothing further transpired.) Following the distribution, Margaritaville will be merged into a subsidiary of Cayo Hueso in a forward triangular merger in which the Margaritaville shareholders will receive Cayo Hueso common stock. Does the subsequent merger affect the validity of treating the distribution as a § 355 transaction? Does your answer depend on whether or not after the post-distribution merger the former Margaritaville Corp. shareholders own at least 50 percent of the outstanding Cayo Hueso Corp. stock?

3. Cayo Hueso Corp. has approached the board of directors of Margaritaville Corp. with an offer to acquire Margaritaville's controlled subsidiary, Conch Corp. Cayo Hueso and Margaritaville have devised the following plan. Margaritaville will distribute Conch to its shareholders pro rata. (Assume that this distribution could have qualified under § 355 if nothing further transpired.) Following the distribution, Conch will be merged into a subsidiary of Cayo Hueso in a forward triangular merger in which the Conch shareholders will receive Cayo Hueso common stock. Does the subsequent merger affect the validity of treating the distribution as a § 355 transaction? Does your answer depend on whether or not after the post-distribution merger the former Conch Corp. shareholders own at least 50 percent of the outstanding Cayo Hueso Corp. stock?

SECTION 4. CONSEQUENCES TO PARTIES TO A CORPORATE DIVISION

1. The stock of Rock of Ages Corp. is owned 60% by Elvis, whose basis for his stock is $1,000,000; 22% by Buddy, whose basis for his stock is $750,000; and 18% by John, whose basis for his stock is $450,000. Rock of Ages has two independent divisions: Classic Rock Compact Disc Division and the New Age Music Video Division. The Classic Rock CD Division has assets with a basis of $1,000,000 and a fair market value of $1,800,000. The New Age Music Video Division has assets with a basis of $1,000,000 and a fair market value of $1,200,000. (Neither division has any liabilities.) Rock of Ages has $2,000,000 of accumulated earnings and profits ($1,200,000 attributable to the Classic Rock CD business and $800,000 attributable to the New Age Music Video business) and a $500,000 net operating loss attributable to its New Age Music Video business.

   (a) Rock of Ages transfers the New Age Music Video business assets to a new subsidiary, New Age Corp., the stock of which it then distributes to its shareholders pro rata.

      (1) Assuming that the transaction qualifies under § 355, what are the tax consequences to the corporations and to the shareholders?

      (2) Assuming that the transaction did not qualify under § 355, what are the tax consequences to the corporations and to the shareholders?

   (b) Rock of Ages transfers the New Age Music Video business assets to a new subsidiary, New Age, the stock of which it then distributes to Buddy and John in exchange for all of their shares of Rock of Ages. Buddy receives 55% of the New Age stock and John receives 45% of the New Age stock.

      (1) Assuming that the transaction qualifies under § 355, what are the tax consequences to the corporations and to the shareholders?

      (2) Assuming that the transaction did not qualify under § 355, what are the tax consequences to the corporations and to the shareholders?

2. San Francisco Dungeness Crab Corp. (SFDC) owned 60 percent of the stock of Cedar Key Clam Farms, Inc. (CKCF); SFDC's basis in the CKCF stock was $300,000. The remaining 40 percent of the stock of CKCF was held by Diane. In January 2011, SFDC purchased Diane's CKCF stock for $1,000,000 in cash. In December 2014, after a dispute among the shareholders, SFDC distributed all of the stock of CKCF to

Earl, one of SFDC's shareholders, in complete redemption of Earl's shares of SFDC to settle the dispute.

(a)(1) What are the tax consequences to Earl and to SFDC?

(2) Would your answer change if SFDC had acquired Diane's CKCF stock in November 2009?

(3) Would your answer change if SFDC had acquired Diane's CKCF stock in January 2011 in exchange for SFDC voting common stock? (Assume that Diane's basis for the CKCF stock was $100,000.)

(b) Suppose that San Francisco Dungeness Crab Corp. (SFDC) had owned 80 percent of the stock of CKCF for more than five years, but purchased the remaining 20 percent from Diane last year for $1,000,000 in cash. This year SFDC distributed CKCF to Earl in redemption of all of his stock. What are the tax consequences to Earl and to SFDC?

3. (a)(1) Prior to January 2010, all of the stock of Aloha Corp. was owned by Akoni, Ema, and Hana. In January 2010, Iolana purchased 30 percent of the stock of Aloha Corp. In December of 2010, Aloha distributed 60 percent of the stock of its previously controlled subsidiary, Waikiki Corp., to Iolana in exchange for all of Iolana's stock of Aloha. The remaining 40 percent of the Waikiki stock was distributed to Hana in redemption of all of Hana's Aloha stock. Assuming that the transaction qualifies under § 355, what are the tax consequences under § 355(d)?

(2) How would your answer differ if Iolana had acquired the Aloha stock in a type B reorganization?

(3) How would your answer differ if Iolana had acquired the Aloha stock in November 2009?

(b) Instead of distributing the Waikiki stock to Iolana and Hana, in December of 2014, Aloha distributed all of the stock of Waikiki Corp. to Akoni and Ema in exchange for all of their stock of Aloha. Iolana continued as a shareholder of Aloha owning 30 shares, and Hana continued as a shareholder of Aloha owning 20 shares. Assuming that the transaction qualifies under § 355, what are the tax consequences under § 355(d)?

SECTION 5. DIVISIVE DISTRIBUTIONS IN CONNECTION WITH ACQUISITIONS

1. Reconsider problem 2. from Section 3. Even if the distribution qualifies under § 355(a), is any aspect of it nevertheless taxable?

2. Reconsider problem 3. from Section 3. Even if the distribution qualifies under § 355(a), is any aspect of it nevertheless taxable?

3. In October of last year, the management of D Corp., which is publicly traded, decided to spin-off C Corp., one of D Corp.'s many operating subsidiaries. C Corp.'s manufacturing operations produced toxic waste and an investment banker had advised D Corp. that divesting itself of C Corp. would enhance the long-run value of D Corp. and provide it with better access to public capital markets. D Corp. completed the spin-off of C Corp. in March. In which, if any of the following circumstances, must D Corp. recognize gain with respect to the C Corp. stock?

   (a)(1) In February of this year, P Corp. approached the D Corp. management with a proposal to acquire D Corp., conditional on the spin-off of C Corp., which was scheduled to occur the following month. D Corp.'s management agreed to consider the offer. In May D Corp.'s management made a counter proposal to P Corp. regarding the terms of the proposed acquisition, and P Corp.'s management agreed to the counter-offer. Following shareholder approval, D Corp. was acquired by P Corp. in August of this year in a reverse triangular merger pursuant to which the D Corp. shareholders received P Corp. stock that constituted 45 percent of the outstanding stock of P Corp.

   (2) Would your answer change if D Corp. shareholder's received P Corp. stock that constituted 52 percent of the outstanding stock of P Corp?

   (b) In January of last year, P Corp. approached the D Corp. management with a proposal to acquire D Corp. In February of last year, D Corp.'s management made a counter proposal to P Corp. regarding the terms of the proposed acquisition, which P Corp. rejected. D Corp. completed the spin-off of C Corp. in March of this year. In October of this year, P Corp. approached the D Corp. management with a new proposal to acquire D Corp., at a higher price than in the proposal made last year, and D Corp.'s management agreed to the offer. Following shareholder approval, D Corp. was acquired by P Corp. in December of this year in a reverse triangular merger pursuant to which the D Corp. shareholders received P Corp. stock that constituted 45 percent of the outstanding stock of P Corp.

(c) In November of last year, P Corp. approached the D Corp. management with a proposal to acquire D Corp. D Corp.'s management agreed to the offer. Following shareholder approval, D Corp. was acquired by P Corp. in January of this year in a reverse triangular merger pursuant to which the D Corp. shareholders received P Corp. stock that constituted 45 percent of the outstanding stock of P Corp.

PART VII

Corporate Attributes in Reorganizations and Other Transactions

CHAPTER 24

Carry Over and Limitation of Corporate Tax Attributes

Section 1. Carry Over of Tax Attributes

1. X Corp. acquired Y Corp. in a type A merger. Immediately before the merger, X Corp. had accumulated earning and profits of $1,000,000 and Y Corp. had a negative accumulated earnings and profits account of $1,100,000. During the year of the merger, neither X Corp. nor Y Corp. had any current earnings and profits. If X Corp. distributes $200,000

to its shareholders after the merger, how much of the distribution is a dividend? Does it matter whether a shareholder always held X Corp. stock or whether the shareholder is a former Y Corp. shareholder who acquired the X Corp. stock in the merger?

2. (a) The year after X Corp. acquired Y Corp. (in problem 1), X Corp. had current earnings and profits of $600,000; it made no distributions. What is it accumulated earnings and profits account at the end of the first year after the merger?

   (b) Alternatively, the year after X Corp. acquired Y Corp. (in problem 1), X Corp. lost $600,000. What is it accumulated earnings and profits account at the end of the first year after the merger?

SECTION 2. LIMITATIONS ON NET OPERATING LOSS CARRYOVERS FOLLOWING A CHANGE IN CORPORATE OWNERSHIP

1. Five individuals, A, B, C, D, and E, each owned 20 percent of the stock of L Corp. At the end of last year L Corp. had a net operating loss carryover (NOL) of $5,000,000. On January 1st of this year, P Corp. bought all of the stock of L Corp. for $10,000,000 in cash. This year, L Corp. made $4,000,000 before taking any NOL into account. On January 1st, thc "long term tax exempt federal rate" was 1 percent.

   (a) What is L Corp.'s taxable income after taking its NOL into account?

   (b) Would your answer differ if instead of P Corp. buying the stock of L Corp. from A, B, C, D, and E, the purchaser had been F, another individual?

   (c) Would your answer differ if instead of P Corp. buying the stock of L, P Corp. had acquired L Corp. in a type B reorganization, giving each of A, B, C, D, and E, $2,000,000 worth of P Corp. common stock?

2. Five individuals, A, B, C, D, and E, each owned 20 percent of the stock of L Corp. Prior to 2010, L Corp. had no NOLs. In 2010 L Corp. incurred an NOL of $10,000,000. Over the past few years, P Corp. has made the following purchases of L Corp. stock.

Selling shareholder		*Purchase Date*
A	20%	6/ 1/2009
B	20%	1/ 1/2010
C	20%	6/30/2012
D	20%	12/31/2012
E	20%	6/30/2013

As of what date does § 382 apply to limit the use of any of L Corp.'s 2010 NOL that is then unused?

3. X Corp. is a closely held start up high technology company. A and B each own 1,000,000 shares. It has an unexpired NOL due to significant R&D deductions under § 174. X Corp. makes an initial public offering of 3,000,000 shares at $15 per share. Does § 382 apply to X Corp. as a result of the IPO?

4. P Corp. owns 80 percent of the stock of L Corp. C, an individual, owns the remaining 20 percent of the stock of L Corp. L Corp. has an unexpired NOL.

   (a) Z Corp. purchased 70 percent of the stock of P Corp. Assuming that C owns no stock of either P Corp. or L. Corp., does § 382 apply to L Corp.?

   (b) Z Corp. purchased 40 percent of the stock of P Corp. Assuming that C owns no stock of either P Corp. or Z Corp., does § 382 apply to L Corp.?

   (c) Z Corp. purchased 70 percent of the stock of P Corp. C owns no stock of P Corp. but C does own 20 percent of the stock of Z Corp., does § 382 apply to L Corp.?

5. Y Corp. owns 51 percent of the stock of L Corp. D, an individual owns 49 percent of the stock of L Corp. D owns 4 percent of the stock of Y Corp. Does § 382 apply to L. Corp. if D purchases all of the L stock owned by Y Corp.?